I
CAN
I
HAVE
I
WILL

Blooming Through Life's
Greatest Tragedies

CASSIDY GLO NOVAK

For speaking engagements, media inquiries, or general information, you may contact the author at CassidyGloNovak@gmail.com or visit CassidyGloNovak.com.

All Scripture quotations, unless otherwise indicated, are taken from the The Holy Bible, New International Version, NIV Copyright 1973, 1978, 1984, 2011 by Biblica, Inc., English Standard Version® ESV Copyright 2001 by Crossway®, New Life Version® NLV Copyright 1986 by Christian Literature Internattional, New International Reader's Version® NIRV Copyright 1996 by by Biblica, Inc., and are used with permission.

Published by Silversmith Press, Houston, Texas.

Silversmith Press titles may be purchased in bulk for educational, business, fundraising, or sales promotional use. For information, please email office@silversmithpress.com.

ISBN 979-8-9873816-1-8 (Softcover Book)
ISBN 979-8-9873816-3-2 (Hardcover Book)
ISBN 979-8-9873816-2-5 (eBook)

Silversmith Press, Houston, Texas–www.SilversmithPress.com
Printed in the United States of America.

SILVERSMITH
PRESS

I would like to dedicate this book to my wonderful children. Cadence, Chloe, Cailynn, Cora and Clayton. I'm so honored to be your mom. I hope this book encourages you on your walk through life. I pray your heart will always be for the Lord, no matter what you face. Trials will come and people will let you down, but God is always faithful. Know that I am always here for you no matter what. I am proud of you and love you very much.

Contents

Thank You..7

Foreword..17

Chapter 1 – Stranger In The Water....................21

Chapter 2 – Re-Birth 39

Chapter 3 – The Road To Recovery...................47

Chapter 4 – Crown Of Righteousness................59

Chapter 5 – An Enchanted Evening...................69

Chapter 6 – Laying The Groundwork.................73

Chapter 7 – A Fairytale Romance......................77

Chapter 8 – Meet Me At The Alter....................87

Chapter 9 – The Nightmare Begins....................93

Chapter 10 – Love Is A Choice.......................105

Chapter 11 – Ready, Set, Grow.......................115

Chapter 12 – It's A Slow Fade: *Clif Tells His Story*....127

Chapter 13 – Out Of The Ashes.....................141

Chapter 14 – Golden Season..........................149

Chapter 15 – The Mystery Diagnosis...............157

Chapter 16 – Don't Waste Your Present............167

Scriptures For Further Reflection 174

About The Author...230

Thank You

First, I'd like to pour out my gratitude to the Lord. He has truly been my Savior time and time again when the enemy has tried to take my life. Thank you, Lord, for walking through every valley with me and giving me hope, a future, and an incredible testimony of your faithfulness. Thank you for your unmerited favor and grace. Thank you for your forgiveness time and time again. Thank you for my many blessings in this life.

Clifton: Words cannot describe how thankful I am for you. You have given me a life I could have only dreamed of. Thank you for being my protector, my leader, my prayer partner, my motivator, and my best friend. Thank you for choosing to stay when the going got tough. Thank you for all you sacrifice every day for our family. Thank you for being the best father our children could ever hope for. Thank you for loving me through all my imperfections and shortcomings. Thank you for being my rock. I love you so!

Cadence: Thank you for always loving on me and giving me the best hugs. On days I feel overwhelmed or down you always pick me up with your love. Thank you for your funny jokes and efforts in our family. I admire you for many things, you are truly brilliant! You inspire me in many ways, and I'm honored to be your mom. I love you Lily-Loo!

Chloe: Thank you for being a fearless warrior. You my dear, are strong and artistic in many ways. I'm amazed by your grace and dancing. I love to see you ride! Thank you for the joy and laughter you bring to our family and all you do to help. It's a blessing to be your mom. I love you Chlo-Glo!

Cailynn: Thank you for your servant's heart and truly caring for others. You have a heart of gold and I'm blessed to watch you blossom and grow. You have the beauty of Esther and a thoughtful heart that always reaches out to comfort and include others. Thank you for all the beautiful letters and gifts you give me often. I'm thrilled to be your mom. I love you Juliet!

Cora: Thank you for being my sweet sunshine every day. You are such a cutie pie and I love having you home to teach you and watch you grow. Thank you for all you do to help our family and all the laughter and joy you bring our home. Thank you for being such a good friend and big sissy to your brother. I adore being your mom. I love you Scootie!

Clayton: Thank you for bringing me a love I had never known before. You are truly my yummy and I love you so much. It is such a joy to watch you be a little man. Thank you for your hugs all throughout the day and telling me "You're the best mommy ever." It's like you know when I need to hear it the most. I'm so happy to be your mom. I love you Bubba!

Mom & Dad: Thank you for walking through some of the darkest moments of my life and never giving up on me. Thank you for being prayer warriors that never faltered in your faith to carry me through the hard times. Thank you for your advice and counsel. Thank you for your words of encouragement and affirmation. Thank you for the Christian heritage you raised me in. Thank you for sowing into my children's lives and all the special things you do for each of them. I'm so blessed to be your daughter, and to call you friend. I am thankful to the Lord every day for you.

Lil & Jerry: Thank you for loving me as a daughter. Thank you for praying fervently for our family. Lil thank you for all the school and many activities you always do with the kids. Thank you for always being willing to help me wherever I need it. Thank you for your encouragement and love. Jerry thank you for all the times you've filled our home with music. Thank you for the songs you've written for the kids. Thank you to both of you for the many thoughtful and generous gifts over the years. Thank you for sowing into our children's lives the truths of The Word of God.

To my Siblings: Thank you for believing in me when I didn't. Thank you for the joy and laughter you bring to my life. Thank you for being great friends. Thank you for your love, support, and prayers throughout the years. I am thankful for the times we have had in worship together. I am thankful for the vacations and memories we have shared from years in past. And I ask the Lord for more cherished moments in the future.

My grandparents (especially my MiMi): What an incredible Christian heritage and legacy you've given to me. Thank you for the wonderful childhood memories and helping me to grow to be the woman I am today. Thank you for your endless prayers and godly counsel. I love you the mostest!

Barbara & Mike: Thank you for helping my ministry in many ways. Thank you for your help with the kids and the rides to and from the airport throughout the years. Thank you for encouraging and praying with me through writing out my life story. Thank you for your counsel, love, and friendship. Thank you for being my prayer partner, and for holding me accountable.

Brian & Ang: Thank you for being the best pastors and friends we could ask for. Can't imagine doing life without you guys. Thank you for the advice, prayer time, and worship sessions. Thank you for helping us grow in many areas of our lives. Ang, you are the best bosom friend I could ask for and I cherish our times together. Thank you for believing in me. Thank you for encouraging me and pouring into my family. Brian, thank you for the beautiful forward you wrote for my book. It means a lot.

Nicole & Phil: Thank you for being the best prayer warriors we could ask for. Thank you for your incredible hospitality and generosity in our friendship. Thank you for loving my kids in extravagant ways. Thank you for pushing me to be my best and to let things go. Thank you for helping me learn to implement healthy boundaries. Nicole, I'm grateful to have you as my spiritual bulldog, and you're an awesome bookend.

Val: Thank you for being a fun bestie. Thank you for the joy you bring my life. Thank you for being iron that sharpens iron and for loving me at my worst. Thank you for encouraging me to invest in my health and your many affirmations in my life. Thank you for helping me grow to be the best wife, mom, daughter, and sister I can be.

Sarah: How do I put into words how thankful I am for you? We've walked through some of the hardest seasons of life with each other, and I am so grateful we could do it together. I think you are an incredible cousin and even better friend. Thank you for dropping everything to help me time and time again. And thanks for making life so fun!

Jeanne & Tracy: Thank you for being the best friends I could ask for walking through the most difficult time of my life. Thank you for the joy and music you bring to my life. Thank you for all the wonderful memories and lifting me up when I was weary and weak. Jeanne, thanks for being an incredible life coach. Tracy, thanks for being my best cheerleader. To both of you, thank you for encouraging and inspiring me in so many ways. Thanks for always being there for me, however I need you. Life is better with you.

Erika & Becky: Thank you for being my dearest friends when moving up North. I was alone and grieving in so many ways and you took me into a friendship beyond what I could hope for. You both have devoted so much love into my life and my children's. Thank you for being there whenever needed, however needed. And thank you for the endless laughter and fun you bring to my life.

Jen & Lauren (Roomies): I'm so thankful to have you as a part of our home and family. Thank you for the pep talks and spontaneous girl time. Thank you for lending a helping hand when I need it and loving our kids. Thank you for the encouragement and account- ability. Thank you for the laughter and chocolate when needed.

Lauren: Thank you for coming back to our friendship and encouraging me to take time for myself and not feel guilty. Thank you for the many trips you have tak- en to see me and for thoughtful gifts given throughout the years. And thank you for all your business savvy advice and supporting my dreams.

Jaime: Thank you for the 30 plus years of soul sis- ter friendship. Some of my favorite memories are with you, hours of prayer time and worship together, and laughter that was healing to the soul. Tru-Luv, it's 5:28, and time for another history mystery. Love you very much.

Ms. R: Thank you for believing in me in so many ways and pushing me to be the best individual I could be. I learned so much from you and became who I am today because of your investment in my life. Thank you for being a great friend and for loving my kids too.

Pastor John & Jennifer: Thank you for taking us into

the Chapel family and loving us. Thank you for believing in my calling and helping my confidence grow in using my gifts for Christ.

Mike & Kathy: Thank you for investing in our marriage from day one. Thank you for your counsel through the years and for dedicating the girls. Thank you for the growth opportunity to be the worship leader at Life Church.

To my many wonderful Aunts: You have been so supportive, loving, and uplifting in my life. Thank you for helping me to see my value and worth and praying for me often. Thank you for the special breakfasts and lunchtimes, and for all the thoughtful cards and gifts throughout the years.

To my many wonderful cousins: Thank you to those who have been there for me to give amazing love, affirmations, support, help, and prayers. Thank you for helping me feel important and loved. Thank you for loving my children and investing in their lives.

Aunt Karen & Uncle Fred: Thank you for being peacekeepers. We appreciate the many times you have lent a helping hand with our home and our children too. Thank you for sharing your wisdom and insight from the Lord. And thank you also for the many thoughtful gifts throughout the years.

Charlana: Thank you for your godly counsel in my life for the past two decades. I appreciate and admire you in many ways. Thank you for your prayers and wisdom.

Sheena: I am thankful for our friendship of over 30 years. What a blessing we reconnected years ago after living states apart. Thank you for your continual affirmations in my life. Thank you for valuing me and my family, it means a lot. Thank you for the prayers and thoughtful gifts. Thank you for believing in my ministry.

Dr. Patel & Amy: Thank you for your help in my healing journey! Thank you for going above and beyond what I could have asked for in my surgery and recovery.

Joanna: Thank you for taking on my book and bringing it to life. Thank you for your encouragement and creative inputs into writing out my story. Thank you for your advice and helping me overcome my fears. I'm thankful the Lord finally had our paths cross.

Chris: Thank you for bringing my vision for the cover to life! Appreciate your encouragement and talent.

Candice Insalaco Studios: Thank you for taking the beautiful pictures for my first book. You do wonderful work! I appreciate your prompt help very much.

Foreword

BRIAN BOUGHER, SENIOR PASTOR
OF THRIVE CHURCH

God's story of what He has done in and through Cassidy's life is nothing but incredible. From miraculous healing, Divine intervention, trauma and restoration, and more, you will see the faithfulness of our God! The highs and lows she and her family have experienced and her ability to seek and find God's face and learn eternal treasures everyone can take hold of are priceless. If you start reading, you won't be able to stop. Far more than a compelling story of a woman of God who overcame, this is the story of how big God is in our lives across all spectrums and detail.

If you are struggling through depression, trial, or trauma, you need to read this testimony of what God does! If you haven't, live long enough and you will, so you might as well read this in preparation. No one gets out of this side of eternity unscathed, it is a matter of how we walk it out. Cassidy has walked through the worst of it with the best of them, and better yet, all while letting God use it to get closer to her Lord.

I have known Cassidy and the Novak family for the better part of a decade now and we have only become deeper family friends. As a matter of fact, she is the only person in my life about whom the Lord told me to tell my wife that they were meant to be friends. It was a God appointment for many reasons, most of which I won't list here for they would probably bore you as a reader. What I can tell you is that this book is filled with the main reasons: Cassidy loves Jesus with her whole heart and seeks Him no matter what comes and won't stop.

Her husband Clif is one of my closest friends and brothers in the Lord and I can tell you that his section of the story, featured within, is equally compelling, convicting, and encouraging. He is one brother I would stand by and within any fire of life and I'm humbled to call him friend. His candor and passion for the Lord is rare in men these days. He's a true man of God. As a matter of fact, the life change that has happened in both him and Cassidy is why we refer so many in our church to them for marriage ministry. Together, they are a powerhouse for God's Kingdom and church. As you may have realized, I have the privilege and honor of being Cassidy's Pastor. She and her family minister in our church near-weekly. We have vacationed with the Novak's, wept with them, laughed with them, and all the other things. They have helped us plant a church for six years. We have gotten to build the Kingdom together. So, when I offer my recommendation, it is from someone who knows the real deal of their story and this is all true and eye-witnessed by many. God has done great things in and through Cassidy's life.

They are who they are without pretense. Their hearts are full of generosity, compassion, and conviction. Yet, what I love most about Cassidy and Clif is what you see in this book. Her desire to see God move in power in every person's life at any given time is unrivaled. There isn't a day you won't be welcomed into their table, regardless of your status. You'll see this in her writing as well. To the very last page of this book, you'll find resources and verses, beyond her story, to help you walk through the fire and walk out in freedom. Cassidy's desire to see you set free to greater degree through God using her story is on display front to back. God wants you delivered, healed, and free, and His heart for that is exemplified in Cassidy's story!

CHAPTER 1

Stranger In The Water

"Breathe, you have to remember to breathe!" The voice grew louder in my head as I struggled to gain consciousness face down in the water. *How did I get here? Is this really happening, or just another nightmare?* I try to move my arms, or anything really, and my body won't respond. I wondered if I was dying. It felt like minutes had past as I lay there completely helpless. Then, out of nowhere I feel someone grab under my arms and hoist me out of the water, almost effortlessly. I desperately gasp as my lungs fill with the warm air. Completely dazed and confused, I look up to see the sun setting on the horizon of the water, and I notice panicked voices shouting my name all around me. I'm not sure what's happening but I can tell they are desperately trying to get me back to the boat. The sound of voices fades off as dark shadows roll over my eyes and I realize I'm blacking out again.

When I come to, I am being carried inside and I hear

someone yelling to call an ambulance, "Did she break her neck?" Someone else yells, "Be careful setting her down!" A friend's mother is there and prays, "Oh Lord help her now, wrap your arms around her." Peace and relief wash over me as a dear friend of the family lays hands on me and starts praying in the spirit. I have no idea what's going on and then I feel it coming on again, extreme nausea, then vomiting, then everything fades away as I lose consciousness and find myself again in complete blackness.

Just hours earlier, I was a carefree college student singing at the top of my lungs while driving with the windows down. My good friend Tracy and I were headed to the lake for a fun-filled day in the sun on Memorial Day, May 31, 2004. It had been a rough year for me as I struggled with my sense of self, questioning my faith in Christ. I was born and raised in a Christian home and my family went to church every time the doors were open. I took my upbringing for granted and allowed the scriptures to become mundane stories to me.

At twenty years old, I had regretfully done some things I never thought I would. And if I'd allow myself to admit it, I was hardened, wounded, and angry. Mainly with myself. Life was not all sunshine. In fact, there were quite a few rainstorms to face. But you need the rain for beautiful flowers to emerge. I had to learn to become better, *not* bitter.

In my life I have faced many tragedies. As many victims of abuse do, I had adapted to keep my horrific experiences concealed. Many children are threatened by their abuser to never tell. The injured try to protect themselves by emotionally hiding the memories, and never facing their actual existence. I also used this coping mechanism to suppress abuse and tragedy. The problem with this strategy is that it doesn't work. Burying the pain inside is like trying to bury a ticking time bomb. It will explode eventually and leave our lives in shrapnel. Trying to ignore the pain only prevents wholeness, healing, and restoration.

Many who know me wonder why I have responded the way I have to certain situations over the years. I've been known for being rather emotional. There is often a root behind an individual's negative behavior or overreactions. Giving grace when we don't know the whole story is always the right answer. Truth is, I was sexually abused as a young child on more than one occasion. It was something I blocked out for years. A traumatizing abuse experience will leave a victim in severe emotional and psychological distress.

The resulting symptoms that come from such trage-dies often include PTSD (post-traumatic stress disor-der) until there can be healing. These symptoms are a result of the body, mind, and emotions trying to regain stability and protection to prevent further distress or abuse. Like many sexually abused victims, I developed defensive responses, and trouble finding my voice to say "no" when abuse kept arising. To this day I strug-gle with the ability to say no to people. Abuse victims often deal with anxiety, depression, and control is-sues. I did.

My first encounter of abuse took place when I was just five years old. At least that was the first time I could remember it. Research shows that in the United States, one in four girls, and one in 13 boys experience sexual abuse under the age of 18. Ninety-one percent of abuse takes place from someone known and trusted by the child, such as a family member. Statistics show over 35% of abuse is re-occurring. From what I can recall personally, I was sexually abused by five dif-ferent individuals throughout my early childhood and adolescence. It may have been more because I know I blacked out many horrific things. I am thankful that a few memories have been confirmed by other individ-uals with the abuse that happened to me. Your mind can play a lot of tricks on you in an attempt to survive. Memories create gaps and inconsistencies. Traumatic events are encoded differently in our brains. Abuse victims face fear, threats, and intense stress, which results in fragmented and impaired memories. In fact, did you know that you can change a young child's memory and even shape their personality till age seven? My memories were eventually confirmed by others who knew of a certain time the abuse had happened to me.

Now that I am a parent, I realize the importance of being approachable to your children. Talk to them *frequently* about these uncomfortable topics. It is not a "one and done" conversation. They need to know they can come to you anytime they feel uncomfortable. You must be intentional to *continually* create a healthy environment to ask them about potential violations, and if anything has happened to them. It is *crucial* they know they will not get in trouble, and, above all, that it is not their fault these things have happened to them.

Now, if you have been a victim of sexual abuse, I am so sorry your innocence was stolen from you. I want you to know you are still valuable and worthy of being cherished and protected. You deserve love. Please find someone trustworthy to share your pain with. Get it out of those hidden dark places so you can walk in freedom. And I implore you to forgive your abusers. They may not deserve your forgiveness, but you deserve the deliverance that comes from forgiving them. Let me say that again, YOU deserve FREEDOM! Get the help you need to heal. It is not weak to need others. We were created for community, and isolation is a dangerous place to be. I encourage you to find a support group or accountability partner to help you on your road to recovery.

By age seven I picked up an anxiety trait known as "pulling." Trichotillomania is a compulsive disorder that involves recurrent, irresistible urges to pull out body hair. I have struggled with pulling out my eyelashes and eyebrows for more than 30 years. It has been a humiliating battle that I have tried to overcome for most of my life. I have often felt it is the first thing people notice about me. I find myself admiring other girls' long eyelashes or perfectly sculpted eyebrows and hated myself that *I* had ruined mine. This anxiety disorder is brought on by stress. For me, it started this when I was going through the abuse as a child, and it escalated in my teen years when I went through my first heart break. First love is so sweet and more so tragic when it comes to an end. Strangely, pulling gave me a sense of control.

While I have come through a lot of healing, even to-day, this disorder can still rear its ugly head when I go through hard situations. I have often woken up with bald spots in my eyebrows and eyelashes that I have created while sleeping. We must deal with our anxiety and the root that is causing it. We can't live in con-demnation that we are somehow to blame for these disorders, convinced that we should be better at over-coming them. That internal turmoil wreaks havoc on anxiety and depression.

Fear, worry, and anxiety are all weapons of Satan to keep us from experiencing the full life that God has for us. These emotions can overwhelm us and keep us paralyzed. Anxiety comes from a root of fear. The Bi-ble tells us 365 times to "fear not." One for each day of the year!

"So do not fear, for I am with you; do not be dismayed, for I am your God. I will strengthen you and help you; I will uphold you with My righteous right hand."

ISAIAH 41:10 NIV

If you have anxiety, I encourage you to seek counsel and find where the root is coming from. If you don't uncover the source and uproot it, it will keep rearing its ugly head. Digging deep is painful, but it is necessary to heal.

There are also chemical imbalances and brain injuries to take into consideration. There are various causes for anxiety. For years, I was trapped in a false belief system that it was wrong to take medication. What if you were born with a hole in your heart? Would you not take a medication to help it function correctly? Sometimes it is necessary and very much needed. Everyone deserves to have quality of life, and our bodies functioning in the capability the Lord designed them to. I do think you need to be very careful what medication you are on and "the why" behind it. But I see no reason for condemnation if you need to be on something to help things function and balance out correctly. When I was put on a small dosage of the correct medication as an adult, it felt like I was breathing correctly within hours of taking it.

By age 14, I developed another PTSD trait; eating disorders, Bulimia and Anorexia Nervosa. Going through the tender transition in puberty, my body image had been greatly skewed in my mind. I believe this was a result of the sexual abuse and self-hatred I was harboring towards my body. I had many insecurities and desperately wanted to be thinner which I thought meant "prettier." The day it all started is fresh in my mind. I had eaten too much and felt miserable, and a small voice inside said, "just throw up to get some relief." So, I did. I bought into the lie that I could eat whatever I wanted and not gain weight if I just got rid of it as soon as possible. I tried many fad diets over the years that seemed to always over promise and under deliver. Eventually I was tired of starving myself, so I quickly fell into the habit of binging and purging. On a typical day, I would hold out on eating food for as long as possible, then I would just snap, knowing I deserved the food. From there, I would go on overload stress eating everything in sight. Then the guilt would come, and the misery of being overstuffed. So, I would drink a ton of warm water and throw up nonstop till I knew there was nothing else left in my stomach.

After a while, I would throw up blood, and would get so dizzy I'd almost pass out. Not my proudest moments. The high that came with the bulimia and pulling was short lived until my next episode or slip up. When we try to self soothe our anxiety, it gives only momentary relief, but it leaves you with regrets and consequences that sometimes last a lifetime. Acting out in sin to try and comfort ourselves, over promises and under delivers every time. I had searched for my worth and security in people and things of the world, only to end up at the roadblock everyone faces, it brings no fulfillment to live a life outside of Christ. Our *true identity* comes from knowing Christ and that we are His joint heir. If we do not find our *true identity* in Him, we will search to no avail in this world and in others.

Proverbs chapter 21 (MSG) states, "If you're addicted to thrills you will have an empty life."

I was empty already and addicted to fake thrills trying to avoid facing my pain. Living for the next social event, shopping spree, date, vacation or promotion, might bring temporary satisfaction, but it will not last. Because our flesh is never satisfied, we need more in our lives. We need the Lord.

That Memorial Day I shifted through my thoughts while we rounded another bend of the lake. What was I doing with my life? The day before at church, I had gone up to the altar and asked God to please soften my heart and reveal Himself to me. As I sat at the altar allowing the music to penetrate the walls of my heart, I felt someone touch the right side of my head. I looked up to see who was trying to get my attention. No one was there. Chills ran up my arms to the back of my neck as I realized no human had touched me. God was letting me know "I am here." I hear soft music playing in the background of my thoughts then it quickly stops.

"Is He here? Is anyone here? Where am I?!"

"Thud!" Someone pounding on my chest brings me to, and I hear the EMT say, "We can't take her back to our hospital, she clearly has head trauma, and our Neurology Department is on strike." The ambulance then takes me to a nearby field where I feel wind hitting my face as they lift me into a helicopter. I feel embarrassed briefly that I've vomited again, this time on one of the men trying to revive me as he shouts, "Stay with me now!" Everything goes quiet and black again.

Often, inconveniences in life can be saving us from something we are not even aware of. The strike of the Neurology Department at the hospital ended up saving my life, causing me to be airlifted to a more specialized medical team. Next thing I know, I'm on a table and look down to see my body convulsing. In some areas, I can feel warm blankets that keep getting changed out to help with the shock. There is pounding again on my chest as the nurses pinch and probe my body to get me to respond and stay awake. But all I can feel are light vibrations. I feel self-conscious as a male nurse cuts off my bathing suit, and I feel someone remove my belly and toe ring. Complete chaos surrounds me, yet I have no idea what is going on? The few moments I was awake, I tried desperately to tell anyone who is near me that something is terribly wrong. But then I realize I am lying in a hospital, so I figure they already know. I can't speak no matter how hard I try anyway.

A younger nurse with dark hair named Erika comes to my bedside and says, "Sweetie you have bleeding and swelling on your brain and they're going to have to operate on you." I recognize her voice and realize I had heard her moments earlier saying, "She has faded over 90 percent in the last 10 minutes! Where is the surgeon? Has anyone been able to reach the family?" Somehow, I mumble my dad's cell phone number. The individuals around my bed stare at me in disbelief for a moment. Someone yells to write the number down, then they go back to prepping me for surgery.

How did I get here? I have flashbacks of the day running through my mind. I remember the excitement of the good weather and a fun day planned with friends. I remember the boat rides, diamond-like sparkle on the water from the sun, the wind blowing through my long blonde hair. Then it hits me, I also remember the stone entrance at the lake house. The same stone entrance that had haunted me in my dreams over the past several months. For a while, many of my family members had been having nightmares about me. I also had a few spiritual dreams that were so disturbing they will forever be engraved in my mind. I told one of my dreams to my parents and my dad sought the Lord for its meaning. Around the time of this dream, my dad was also led to pray for me and fast for *ten* days. There were many details with warnings my dad felt he received from the Holy Spirit for me. One of those being: if I ever saw a stone entrance, like the one I saw in my dream, I was to flee for my *physical life*. Many had felt all these nightmares had been concern of my *spiritual death*, but this one was different. That day as Tracy and I pulled up to our friend's lake house, I saw the stone entrance and felt a check in my spirit, but then quickly pushed it aside rationalizing it all in my mind. After all, we weren't doing anything wrong. *What harm would come from being with a good Christian family?*

Those little nudges from the Holy Spirit are so vital to obey and listen to closely. Even when it makes no sense to you, even when you are going against everyone else's opinions to stand alone—do it!

As I lay there, more moments came to mind. The water sport activities, many of which I had done for years, hydro sliding and tubing. The flash backs came in pieces. I remembered going around the lake one last time before sun set, the other tubers falling off, the boat turning around, and then me falling off my tube and bouncing three times. That third time was when I hit something hard. Whatever I hit literally shook my brain. Growing up, I had taken several falls off my horses, and had head injuries with cheerleading over the years, but never had I hit my head this hard. Then, yellow and purple lights flooded my eyes along with a very loud, distorted ringing.

About twenty miles north of where I was lying in the hospital, my parents, Bruce and Gail, were on the road. My parents were very firm in teaching godly principles. They had sacrificed much in their lives to make a wonderful home and upbringing for my siblings and myself. I had a blessed childhood in numerous ways. We lived a fortunate life that many others desire, but never have. As any teenager might, I had butted heads with them over the years while trying to gain my own independence. I knew my parents loved me unconditionally and saw my full potential, but due to their strictness, and me being in trouble often, on top of the shame from my abuse they were unaware of, I felt like I was a big letdown and burden to them. I believed a lie from the enemy that I needed to earn their love, or anyone's love. I've struggled with approval addiction most of my life and being a people-pleaser. This is a vicious cycle of inner chaos and striving to be the best I can be for everyone else, and not get anyone upset. Believing these lies from the enemy made me over-reactionary. I had been known to make life rough at times with my dramatics. And I hated myself that I was known for this. Why couldn't I just be a better person? My family even had family meetings to try and help me, but they didn't know how. My mom shared with me later it was terrible to watch me so miserable going through life; she didn't know why and didn't know how to help me.

When they got the first call from the hospital and started driving an hour and a half to Orlando, my parents assumed they were coming to pick me up with a simple injury, and they would wrap me in a blanket and take me home. They were maybe even a little annoyed and concerned by the fact that I was airlifted, and we had no form of medical insurance. This would be a very expensive concussion. My parents were quite taken back when more phone calls started coming in. First, it was the nurse Erika, "Have you been notified of your daughter's accident? Are you on your way?" Then another call from a chaplain, "Where are you? Your daughter is in critical condition." My mom turned to my dad as they both realized this was a lot more serious than they thought. They grabbed hands and asked God to hold me, and almost immediately peace came over them both.

Back at the hospital, down the hall from where I was Dr. Smith picked up the phone to dial. He was a tall man with dark, longer hair and no bed-side manner. However, his melancholy perfectionism made him the best at what he did. My father answered and Dr. Smith proceeded to explain that I had a ½ inch blood clot covering the entire right side of my brain, growing by the minute.

"Sir I need your permission to operate."

"Can you wait so we can pray with her, we are only about ten minutes away."

"No if we don't operate on your daughter within minutes she will die."

He explained that head injuries have what is called a *golden hour.* This is the period immediately after a traumatic brain injury during which there is the highest likelihood that prompt medical treatment will prevent death. Time was running out.

As the medical team rushed me down the hallway, I felt like I was having an out of body experience watching everything in slow motion as I was pushed quickly to the operating room. Inexplicably, a strange peace came over me, almost an eerie stillness of my body and soul surrendering. I silently prayed for the Lord to forgive me of any sins, and to hold my family in His hands. Then I looked up and saw a butterfly on the ceiling, and an intense light overtook me.

CHAPTER 2

Re-Birth

Suddenly, everything stopped. I could no longer hear anyone around me, or even myself breathing. I was aware, and so alone.

It's the little things in life you take for granted and miss the most when they are gone. A simple clock ticking assures you there is still time. A hot bubble bath, a Sunday nap, the embrace of someone you love, warm chocolate chip cookies, the smell of a newborn baby, the sunrise and sunset; I would have given anything to experience any one of those in that moment. It's ironic to me that my life was almost taken at my favorite time of day, sunset. It is such a peaceful transition time every day when everything becomes still and quiets down for a time of rest. The scripture says that God walked with Adam in the cool of day. The promise of a fresh start, a new beginning, that's what I see when I look up at a painted dusk sky. Another sign of new beginnings is the butterfly representing re-birth or new life. And that is exactly what the Lord reassured me of as I looked up and caught a glimpse of a painted butterfly as I was rolled into surgery.

On that fateful Memorial Day, I was embracing the beauty of the sunset and in an instant, everything changed. Life is so unpredictable, and that is why it's crucial to live every moment like it could be your last. Isn't it so typical to think the horrors in life won't happen to us, that we are somehow invincible? I was guilty of this mindset; of thinking I was a good person and would be spared from the tragedies others face in life. Looking back now, I realize it's a huge blessing that I have faced and gone through these trials and tribulations. As I write out my life and see the chapters climbing to the climax of my story, I see how these moments have molded me into the character the Lord intended for me to be.

James 1:2-4 NIV states: "Consider it pure joy, my brothers and sisters, whenever you face trials of many kinds. Because you know that the testing of your faith produces perseverance. Let perseverance finish its work so that you may be mature and complete, not lacking anything."

Life is unfair. If you can understand this from an early age, you will do yourself a favor. However, just as life is full of disappointments, God is faithful. He cannot lie. He will never leave our side. And we can become the best versions of ourselves, walking through the pain with him, becoming better instead of bitter.

Ask yourself: *Am I living my life to its fullest potential? Am I investing in other's lives around me and instead of being focused on myself? Am I doing everything in my power to mend fences in relationships with strife and wounds? Am I quickly forgiving those who have hurt me? Am I reaching out and humbling myself to the individuals I have offended, even if not intentionally? Am I honoring everyone in my life, even those who have mistreated and used me? Those who failed to protect me, and those who continue to hurt me?* Now is the moment to choose forgiveness and love. You are not promised tomorrow. Act now and live your life with no regrets.

Six hours is a long time when you are waiting to hear if your daughter will survive. My parents spent their time pacing the hallways in prayer and making phone calls. Waiting and leaning on God's promises during a crisis is where true character is revealed.

Proverbs 24:10 MSG states, "If you fall apart in a crisis, there wasn't much to you in the first place."

My parents were shocked to find out how fast the word had spread about my accident, and how many prayer lists my name was already on. My siblings were flooded with phone calls as well. Some calls came in before they even knew I had been hurt!

My brother Brian is a great husband, father, and a godly man. We had faced some challenges with understanding each other throughout the years, but the Lord has brought us closer through the trials of life. Brian could not relate to me or understand me for a long time. I think I was hard for him to be around me due to our different personalities. The Lord has worked in his heart and life in beautiful ways of bringing empathy for others. I admire him and his wife Becky for so many things, they accept and love *everyone*. They have an approachable nature and are not critical of others. When the Lord brought Becky into our lives, I was grateful because she was the best sister-in-law anyone could ask for. She took me under her wing the moment we met. Becky has been a wonderful example to me over the years of what a godly wife and mother should be. As they both lay awake in silence on that Monday night, Becky turned to Brian and said "Should we just pack up and go? I don't think we are going to get any sleep tonight."

Just down the street my sister Christa and her husband JT were also up and came to the conclusion that they wanted to be present at the hospital offering support for our family as well. Christa is a wonderful older sister who always looks out for my best interest wanting to protect me from any harm in the world. She is a determined individual, strong in her convictions and views. She and I are night and day different, and our relationship has gone through some growing pains. Through our differences though, there is a mutual respect and I admire many things about her, one being her loyalty and decision to always stand by her family. My sister has a faith that never wavers. I esteem many of her God given attributes.

Though JT wanted to go as well, he needed to stay back for work, so Brian, Becky, and Christa started the drive to Orlando. Christa began to be gripped with fear as phone calls flooded in of people asking about my accident. She silently wondered, *What will we do if we lose her? What if she doesn't make it through the surgery?* She felt the emotion welling up in her throat, and she quickly tried to push the thoughts aside and focus on the road.

Upon arrival to Orlando, everyone was in a daze as they waited for the neurosurgery to be complete and hear the results from the doctor.

After surgery, I slowly regained consciousness and

took a deep breath. Immediately there was a burning, stinging sensation that started in my throat and went all the way down to my lungs. My throat felt raw. I ached all over like I had been hit by a train and dragged several miles down the tracks. Then there was the beeping from all the machines around me. I heard air compressing in and out and felt machines compressing my legs. I opened my eyes to see where I was, but everything was so fuzzy, I couldn't focus on anything. Not to mention the agonizing pain in my head the moment the light hit my eyes. I was experiencing pain on a level I'd never felt before, but one thing was for sure, I was alive–and grateful.

Dr. Smith went to the waiting room to address my parents just moments before I was rolled out of post-op into the hallway. He warned them, "Nothing is certain yet. Your daughter probably won't recognize anyone, and she will most likely have problems talking or remembering things. But it is already a huge milestone that she woke up from the extensive surgery and did not go into a coma."

Dr. Smith proceeded to explain the details of my injury which consisted of a ½ inch blood clot covering the entire right side of my brain. In surgery, he had cut through the right side of my skull to remove the hemorrhage and placed my skull back together with five pinwheel plates and over 20 screws. As he finished he said something truly remarkable, "Mr. and Mrs. Ballard, it's amazing that he skull wasn't completely caved in. It's as if she was wearing a motorcycle helmet." I believe with all my heart that the day before the accident, when I was at the altar and felt a touch on my head, that it was the Lord placing a supernatural helmet of protection on me. My dad turned to my mom and said, "God's hand has been on Cassidy from the beginning, and He will not leave or forsake her now." My mom nodded in agreement, then they turned to see me being rolled down the hallway towards them.

Next thing I know I see my mom and dad rushing down the hallway to my bedside. My first thought is to reassure them I am not being dramatic this time or overemotional about my pain. I strain to focus on their faces and speak. Very slowly the words come, "Dad I'm really hurt this time; I'm not crying wolf."

My parents turn to Dr. Smith who was practically shocked. I was alive, I was awake, I could speak, and I knew who my family was—a miracle.

CHAPTER 3

The Road To Recovery

At first, my family was surprised and relieved to see me doing so well right after surgery. Even amazed that I was acting like my old self and joking around. Little did anyone know how hard the next few days would be for all of us.

As the day after my surgery went on, my progress quickly altered. My body began to seize every few minutes, and my mind was triggered to gasp for air often. I was placed on a breathing machine to regulate the amount of oxygen I was getting, and I had a tube draining fluid and blood from my brain. This came out of the right side of my head, resting down by my right shoulder. Those first few days are foggy and hard to remember, which really is a blessing. I think our minds allow us to forget a certain amount of the stress and pain we go through in traumatic situations. Having someone saw through your skull and drill holes into it leaves pain you can't imagine. It was a helpless feeling to have no control over my body and such trouble communicating at times.

My parents forewarned my siblings with the changes that had taken place since the day before when they saw me.

They were coming back the next day to visit me, but I don't think anything could have prepared them to see me in that state I was in. When Christa walked in and saw me struggling to breathe, hooked up to so many machines and wires, she literally started to pass out. Christa turned to Becky who grabbed a hold of her arm to help steady her as she saw the blood leave her face. I knew I must have looked rough but couldn't do much before the next seizure hit me. I soon developed a rash from the morphine, and with the compression cuffs on my legs to prevent blood clots, I was completely miserable, sweating and itching constantly.

JT came back with Christa the next afternoon when he was able to get off work. When he walked into my room and saw me, he told me he loved me for the first time. I will always remember that moment. I didn't know he truly cared until then. I started to cry and felt comforted beyond words. He has become one of my biggest advocates over the years and is a brother I can rely on in any way I need him. JT is always quick to help and offer a hand when needed. He is a great husband, father, son, and brother. I am truly grateful that he is part of our family.

When Becky and Brian came up after work that next day, they too were shocked to see how much my condition had changed in a matter of hours. It was a reality check that I had been in a life-threatening accident and had a long road of recovery ahead of me. As Becky sat at my bedside her eyes grew wide to see the draining tube on my shoulder full of blood, fluid, and literally pieces of brain tissue floating around in it. JT said when the nurses would change it, the smell of death filled the room.

Throughout my stay in the hospital, I asked my family to read the Bible to me frequently. One afternoon while my brother Brian was reading to me, I felt someone kiss me on my forehead. I opened my eyes and asked Brian, "Did you just kiss me on the head?" He shook his head no from the chair he was sitting in across the room. I believe it was my guardian angel, or Jesus Himself.

There were moments when I couldn't even process my thoughts to form sentences. My family witnessed me praying out loud in the spirit when there were no words that I could speak. They also refused to believe

I would be another statistic, even though I had one of the most severe cases of brain injury. They spoke and prayed the promises of the Word of God with every new diagnosis I received. There is power in our words, and we all stood on what we knew—God has the final say.

After about five days, I was evaluated by specialists who determined that upon leaving the hospital, I would need to go to brain rehab for several weeks or months to relearn basic things. It was on this same day that I was desperately trying to feed myself and couldn't even get the spoon to my mouth. I couldn't go to the bathroom on my own or do any simple task. It was very frustrating for me; I felt weak and helpless. It's hard to lose control over your own body. I have a strong, choleric personality and I felt completely helpless.

In the Bible, we read about purifying silver and gold by placing it in fire to draw out impurities. Metal specialists explain that when the metals are placed in the fire and melted down to a liquid state, to the point they are almost ruined in the high heat. But the way they know the liquid is purified and ready to come out of the fire is when you can see your reflection in the metal. I too felt like I was in the fire. I soon realized this was the Lord starting to work out the dross in my heart and mind. This tragedy ended up bringing deep wounds to the surface that I desperately needed healing from. He was purifying me through all of this.

On day six, things started to look brighter. It was a Sunday and churches all over the world were praying for me. I felt a surge of strength, and with my dad's help I was able to get out of my hospital bed and walk around the hospital floor where I was staying. I saw butterflies on the ceiling and told my parents about my encounter with one just before my surgery. From that moment on, butterflies became one of my favorite things to symbolize my life. Like a butterfly coming out of a dark, lonely, cocoon, I was coming into a new beginning. I was starting a new life that the Lord had given to me. I would live like there was no tomorrow.

On the seventh day, I was released from the hospital and sent to a rehab facility to be evaluated and to relearn how to do everyday things. It was a huge wake up call to walk in and see other patients sitting in wheelchairs with the same horse-shoe shaped incision on their heads. They were unable to walk on their own or communicate well. The Lord had truly done something miraculous in my life, and I had much to be thankful for.

While at rehab, I had to go off the IV medications which made the pain almost unbearable. One afternoon a nurse came in to evaluate me and asked what my pain level was on scale of 1-10, I told her a 13 and I meant every bit of it. I had been on so many different medications while in the hospital that my veins had literally eroded away. Every vein in my arms and hands had been used and I was left with massive bruises that lasted for several weeks after. I often wonder what people thought seeing me out in public with all these bruises and my head shaved with a 12-inch scar. I'm sure I was quite the sight to behold!

A few of my good friends and my grandmother Mimi, picked out beautiful scarves and hats for me to wear until my hair could grow back. I got a small glimpse of what cancer patients must feel like. You just want to be normal, feel normal, look normal, after everything traumatizing that you have been through. The "normal" I was trying to get back to entailed lots of testing and what felt like grueling activities. I was determined to pass everything with flying colors, and to get home as quickly as I could. Resting and healing ended up being harder than I thought. It was impossible to sleep at rehab due to the screaming from patients all night long waking up and not remembering where they were.

My roommate hardly could speak, and I remember feeling sad for her that she rarely had anyone coming to visit her and had no flowers or cards. I had such an overabundance of flowers, balloons, and cards, that I asked my mom if we could give her some of mine to brighten up her day. I think it touched her heart. She smiled and nodded at me the best she could from her wheelchair.

I was beyond excited when the day came that I could finally take a shower! Granted, it was sitting on a stool in a tiny shower room, but it was a shower, nonetheless. I sat and let the hot water flow over me for an hour trying to let it soothe my sore joints and muscles. I also tried to wash the crusted blood out of the remainder of my hair on the left side of my head. I had to wash very carefully and not get my 48 sutures wet. We didn't want any chance of infection on such a large open wound, especially so close to my brain. It was the next morning that the sutures came out. This was a painful experience since my skin had started to grow and bond to some of the rope-like threading. Then in its place, I had bright orange iodine rubbed all over the incision, now I truly looked like an Indian warrior! It was one step closer to recovery though, a step I was happy to take.

While in therapy, I had the chance to reflect on the people who had dropped everything to come sit with me, pray with me, and show their love and support. It showed my family who really cared and made the effort to be there. "They" say that if you could attend your own funeral, you'd be surprised at who was on the front row, who stood in the back, and the ones who didn't come at all. I had a small glimpse of this. There were individuals who came to support my family and myself that I never would have thought I could count on. But they were there however needed, to help anyway they could.

My grandparents were a huge support in my recovery and never stopped believing for my complete healing. They have played a major role in my life, and all four of them were incredible individuals, and strong in their faith. They have given me a strong Christian heritage that I will always be thankful for. I learned much from them over the years, and I am thankful I had all four with me for counsel until my adult years. I know their prayers delivered me from many harmful situations, including this life-threatening injury. Never underestimate the power of prayer.

Then there were other friends and family that I thought for sure would be there for me, that never even came to see me once. In the crises of life, we learn who we can rely on, and who our fair-weather friends are.

"One who has unreliable friends soon comes to ruin, but there is a friend who sticks closer than a brother."

PROVERBS 18:24 NIV

I had some incredible friends who drove me around when I could not drive due to seizures. Others spent endless hours helping me with schoolwork so I could pass my college courses (I had to re-learn how to read extensively again). Each of these friends helped me gain back my confidence after everything I had known was shaken to its core, you know who you are...and I will be forever grateful to you for your love and devotion. You were the hands and feet of Christ in my life. Those of you who helped me through my recovery and its different stages, I can't thank you enough!

I love the saying from Eleanor Roosevelt: "Yesterday is history. Tomorrow is a mystery. Today is a gift, that's why we call it the present."

Prayers and hard effort paid off. At the rehab facility, I soon tested above my age with every test they threw my way. While I was at rehab, a specialist explained to me that my *gasping for air* episodes in the hospital, came from my memory continually triggering back to being in the water, and the need to breathe. It was nice to put the puzzle pieces together of the accident and learn the cause and effects of numerous details. The brain is an intricate and incredible organ. Most individuals deal with memory loss after severe brain injury. Ironically, my brain uncovered suppressed memories from my past.

Only three days after being in rehab, a nurse picked up the phone and called my parents telling them, "Mr. and Mrs. Ballard we are calling with great news. Your daughter has excelled in all her tests, and you can come take her home! There is no reason to keep Cassidy here any longer."

My family and I were ecstatic! Only *ten* days after my accident I was going home! The *exact* amount of time that my dad had recently fasted with prayer on my behalf.

I am thankful for the special closeness I shared with my family during the time frame of my accident and recovery. I had thought my family was judging me and disappointed in me for years. Going through this accident helped me to realize I was viewing *myself* that way, and assuming others were as well.

When we learn to love and accept ourselves, we then learn how to accept love from others as well.

CHAPTER 4

Crown Of Righteousness

On the drive home I was terrified. Everything was so bright outside. All the other cars zoomed by. Normal paced things in life were too intense for me now that all my senses were heightened from my injury. Even coming home was nerve racking for me. I felt vulnerable like a young child. I asked my mom and dad if I could sleep on the floor in their room. I stayed there for several nights afraid to be alone. I had lost all confidence and sense of security in my life. I had stared death in the face, and it definitely affected me in more ways than one.

Looking back, I realize I did not receive the emotional healing or professional help I needed going through this brain injury, the horrific pain, facing death, and the draining recovery.

I was the walking miracle! I had nothing I should complain about, right? I was given a second chance when so many are not so fortunate. That was what was engraved into my inner being. And I never dealt with all that I had faced. My entire existence had been wrecked! I needed help! Not to just put on a smile that I was a miracle, everything is wonderful, and that's it. Be happy, be grateful, do your best, and don't forget to smile.

I knew I had been permanently changed. I was a different version of myself. There was a shift in my personality, and I honestly had no idea who I was anymore. In some ways that was a terrifying realization, and every time that new reality arose, I would suppress it and quickly move on. Head injuries can affect just about everything in a person's life.

I slowly got back to the "normalcy" of life. I went back to college just two months after my accident. Dr. Smith strongly suggested I attempt only one class that year. But to keep my scholarships, I needed to go back as a full-time student. That meant taking five courses. Too much pressure indeed for someone going through recovery. With much prayer, tears, long nights of re-reading pages over and over to get the information to sink in, my perseverance paid off and I passed every one of those classes. My parents stood by my side encouraging me where they knew how. They also helped with my bills during that time, and I am very appreciative of that. If only I could have allowed myself to be vulnerable and real rather than wearing a mask that I was "okay."

The summer following my accident, Florida was hit with four hurricanes, leaving us without power for weeks at a time. During one hurricane, about three months after my surgery, I had to go into the ER due to infection in my tonsils. My throat was so swollen I was struggling to breathe. I went in soon afterward to have them removed and the doctor said it was the worst case he had seen in his 40 years of practice. I had three abscesses in my tonsils, and surgery ended up taking twice as long as expected in order to cauterize the wounds. We soon found out I was allergic to the pain medication, and I spent the entire night after surgery vomiting. You can only imagine how miserable that was, and on top of that we had no power, in the summer, in Florida. That summer was not the best for me!

But there were good surprises too through all of this. One day about six months after my accident, I received an unusual phone call from a local beauty pageant director asking me to be a contestant. I wasn't too sure about the whole idea, especially still lacking any confidence in my appearance. I had decided to go ahead and shave my whole head, and my hair was just starting to grow out again. I had a short, punk rock look at the time. After thinking it over for some time, my mom had a unique perspective on it as she told me, "You know Cassidy, this might be a great opportunity from the Lord for you to get your story out, and to share that God is still performing miracles today." I was intrigued and agreed to run for the title of "Miss Silver Springs." A few weeks later, I was nervously standing backstage about to walk out so they could announce the winner. I glanced around at the other girls, some of them whom had been performing in pageants for years. Then I looked out at the audience and felt peace and confidence rise within me. I stepped out into the spotlight knowing the anointing of God was on me. There were blinding lights, cameras flashing, and the audience clapping and cheering. Then the announcement: "And your new Miss Silver Springs 2004 is Cassidy Glo Ballard!" Then they laid it on my head, my crown of righteousness. What an honor. How great is our God that He graced my head with beautiful jewels to cover up my scar.

"But you are the ones chosen by God, chosen for the high calling of priestly work, chosen to be holy peo-

ple, God's instruments to do his work and speak out
for him, to tell others of the night-and-day differ-
ence he made for you-from nothing to something,
from rejected to accepted."

1 PETER 2:9-10 MSG

He allowed me to win a beauty pageant when I felt I had no credentials or confidence to enter. I knew then, while I may be nothing without Him, I could be anything with Him!

Because I won the local pageant title, I was now going to be a contestant in Miss Florida for Miss America. Preparation, preparation, and more preparation came as the weeks grew closer. I was on information overload and training overload. I was up early working out with a personal trainer almost every morning, then worked a full day, and closed out each day with night classes. To say the days were long is an understatement! It was exhausting, but a great way to get me back in shape, and to my normal fast pace of life that I used to know before my accident.

There was a lot of pressure on me from my pageant directors to be thinner, sing better, walk straighter, smile bigger, talk politically correct, and carry myself with poise. Looking back now, I feel the way I was treated was somewhat insensitive--by one director in particular. She knew I had struggled with an eating disorder and low self-esteem for many years. She also knew that I had been through a life-threatening accident less than a year before, yet she still picked me apart at times. I am sure she meant well, and was trying to push me to excellence, but when someone has struggled with serious health issues, I feel they should be handled with more empathy.

I am grateful for the preparation I had in high school for this pageant. In fact, I want to take a moment to thank an individual who believed in me and helped me grow in numerous ways to prepare me for my future. Ms. R was hands down the best teacher and mentor I have ever had. She instilled a wealth of knowledge into my life and believed in me. Thanks to Ms. R, I learned all about business, and came up with my own business plan to implement during high school. I was busy running errands among other things, and she was always a faithful customer. Ms. R nominated me for the award *Who's Who Among American High School Students* and started an *Academy of Entrepreneurship* that I was the first to graduate under. I also became a member of the school club *Future Business Leaders of America* which she led at our school. From this club, I participated in statewide competitions and placed 1st in the state of Florida for interviewing. I met a lifelong friend in these business classes, Lauren. She has gone onto being very successful in the marketing world and has been helpful to me with insight and business strategies.

During some of my roughest patches of emotional struggles in high school, Ms. R never gave up on me. She blessed me with an heirloom ring for my high school graduation. She always encouraged me even when I didn't believe in myself. I didn't think I was valuable, but she saw something in me and made great deposits in my life. To this day, she is still involved in my life, and now my children's lives as well. I'm thankful for our friendship that has grown over the years. Her teaching and guiding helped me prepare for me future. I believe we are strategically placed in people's lives. You may be playing an important life in someone's life without even knowing it. Take the time to invest in others.

I was grateful for my training in interviewing and soared through my mock interviews. I also spoke at events across the community on my platform *"There can be miracles when you believe."* However, I was learning I had little to no control on what I spoke about or what I did. Everything had to be "by the book "or "politically correct" to not offend anyone. I was becoming frustrated because my whole purpose for participating in the pageant world was to touch lives and share how the Lord had healed me, and I was being directed away from that. But I didn't want to quit. I have never been a quitter and knew the Lord had put me in this position for a reason, so I would give it my best shot.

I soon began driving over an hour each way to work with a voice coach on the song I was singing for my talent. I've always had confidence in my voice, but now that had been picked apart as well. On top of that, I was handed a Broadway song to sing that was completely out of my range. The song's lyrics I liked, because it talked about "defying gravity" which I perceived to mean overcoming the odds against you. I knew nothing of the show that the song came from, and looking back now, I wish I had done my research. I feel the song had no anointing when I sang it. If I could do it over again, I would choose my own song to sing, giving credit where credit is due.

Don't let anyone else convince you to be someone you are not. Don't let them pressure you into doing things you are not comfortable with. They won't have to live with your choices, but you will. Don't let others define you. Define yourself.

Even though I was crazy busy, I still made it a point to attend church on a regular basis. And it was on a Wednesday evening that our assistant Pastor Mike announced he would be moving to Chicago to start a church. I felt the Lord press on my heart that I would one day be a part of that church and help with the ministry. I went home and shared this with my parents and my mom said, "We don't know anyone in Chicago." This was true, but we all prayed together about it just the same.

After speaking at a graduation ceremony one evening, I drove to Orlando for a bachelorette party for one of my closest friends Jeanne. I had been asked to be a bridesmaid a few months back, and knew it was my duty to attend the party, even though I was completely exhausted. My parents even encouraged me to go saying the break from my intense routine would do me some good. That night, March 17, 2005, forever changed my life. On this night, I met my soulmate, the man with whom I would spend the rest of my life.

CHAPTER 5

An Enchanted Evening

A group of my closest girlfriends, Jeanne, Tracy, and me, headed to dinner at a fancy restaurant, then it was off to meet up with the groom and his groomsmen for some fun and dancing. When the limo picked us up after dinner, there were already people inside, and the music was blaring. We hopped in and then I felt this strange feeling come over me–an urgency to turn around. When I did, I locked eyes with a handsome groomsman. His eyes were piercing blue which stood out against his dark hair. He was just the right height, tall with strong arms to make you feel feminine and safe when standing next to him. My heart skipped a beat. This was no usual attraction of "boy meets girl." Something stirred in my soul. I knew something was different about this one. He smiled with irresistible dimples, and I immediately felt a surge of confidence and smiled back. It became my mission that night to find out who this guy was. We were drawn to each other, as if we were having our own conversation with just our eyes. I was enchanted to meet him as I found out his name was Clif. Clifton Matthew Novak to be exact, soon to become my best friend, my partner in life, and my soulmate. And guess where he was from? Chicago.

We spent the next couple days getting to know each other, talking for hours around wedding preparations for our friends. Coincidentally, Clif and I were paired to walk together in the bridal party, and I beamed with pride to be on his arm in front of everyone. He had quickly swept me off my feet in just a short time of getting to know him. I soon realized he was falling for me too when we started to walk me down the aisle and he whispered to me, "This may be the first time I am walking you down the aisle, but it won't be the last." I jokingly teased back "What?! We've only just met, aren't you confident!" Clif turned to me smiled with a sparkle in his blue eyes and said, "I'm confident in what the Lord has placed on my heart." I melted. My heart was spoken for from that moment on. Never again would it be swayed to the right or left. I had found the one I was to spend the rest of my life with, the one I was created for.

I came home after the wedding and told my parents about Clif. My dad told me later, that when I walked away, he turned to my mom and said, "That is the man she is going to marry." He shared this with me right before he walked me down the aisle on our wedding day.

Clif changed his return flight after the wedding so he could stay a couple extra days to get to know me better. The days passed quickly, and it was soon time for him to fly back to Chicago. I had a peace about the whole situation, and I knew this wasn't just a wedding weekend crush, and that I would see him again. I hoped it would be soon. As I walked with him to the security lines at the airport to say goodbye, I had to fight back tears, I didn't want him to go. There was so much I wanted to know about this man, so much I wanted him to know about me. But the reality was he lived over a thousand miles away. Clif kissed me and turned to leave with my heart. And thus began our long-distance relationship.

With Clif's birthday being only a day away, I picked out a card that said, "just enough" and sent it to him overnight so he would know I remembered, and I was thinking of him. We talked on the phone for hours every day, starting that first night he went home. Our communication lines were open, and we discussed everything under the sun from politics, religion, raising children, past relationships, and future dreams. We both had come out of serious relationships. Having hours to talk in our long-distance relationship helped build a firm foundation for us. We started devotions and praying together over the phone. It didn't take long to see his face again, in fact less than two weeks later, he was back on a plane to see me. The point of this trip was to confirm everything we already knew. That we were meant to spend the rest of our lives together.

I told everyone in the weeks and months that followed, "I have stopped looking at any other guys, because I have found God's best for me." Many were speculative, but we soon proved our love to them all. We had a God-given agape love that would grow over time. Little did we know how much it would be tested by fire.

CHAPTER 6

Laying The Groundwork

Back to reality, away from my love life, the time crunch was on for the Miss Florida pageant. I was put on a strict diet and schedule of checking in and calling my pageant directors throughout each day and before bed every night. Part of me wanted to "place" at Miss Florida, the other part of me wanted to move on and start my future with Clif. I guess I was feeling a bit torn, especially now that "all that glitters" wasn't so glamorous behind the scenes. However, I was very grateful I had met some wonderful friends in the pageant scene. In fact, one of my coaches, Kelli, and I became quite good friends. I feel she helped me in more ways than one, especially when I was stressed and feeling down about myself due to all the scrutiny. Kelli helped me see the light at the end of the tunnel and encouraged me to press on through each new task thrown my way. Kelli would even come early to the gym and work out with me. I really enjoyed any one-on-one time we had together. I feel the Lord brought about our friendship, and I was honored to be able to help and encourage her through some struggles she was facing as well.

The pageant quickly approached and all the last-minute things to do were piling up. I was excited and nervous that Clif was coming to watch me in the pageant. What if he thought I couldn't compare to all the other girls? I was already feeling insecure about myself before I even got to Miami. Not a good way to start a competition. After meeting my roommate for the week, I felt some relief. She was sweet and we cliqued immediately. Ashley and I still refer to each other as "roomies" and she was the best one I could have asked for at Miss Florida. I performed well considering all the odds that were against me that week. Intimidation was staring me down from every angle. One of my evening gowns ended up torn–or maybe intentionally cut–backstage. I developed a horrible sore throat, and my singing was strained. Even though there was opposition, I believed the Lord guided my steps to be there. The day I arrived, I was amazed that several of the other contestants already knew who I was and had heard about my story. Some of the girls even asked me to pray with them about family or friends going through hard times or asked what scriptures I recommended. I was even asked to lead a group prayer on opening night which I felt very honored to do. I met some amazing women there, some of them I've even kept in touch with over the years.

After all was said and done, I did not place in the pageant. I felt relief it was all over, but tremendous rejection and criticism flooded my mind and heart knowing I had "failed." Even to this day, I sometimes feel defeated about it. I know it was amazing to make it as far as I did to even get to go to Miss Florida, and I must continually ignore the lies of the enemy telling me "You weren't good enough." In my heart I know the reality of it all is that the Lord had His hand on me and was probably protecting me by not allowing me to go any further in the pageant system. Everything happens for a reason; I am a firm believer in that.

I had experienced His protective "no" before. A couple of years prior to the pageant, I was part of a singing group with my childhood best friend, and we had a manager in New Jersey. We had some incredible experiences meeting with top industry executives and singing around Philadelphia, New Jersey, and New York. When the opportunity arose to be signed to a label, my best friend quit and wanted to go back home. I was devastated and felt like I was jilted at the altar. Looking back now, I see God's hand of protection over me in this situation in numerous ways. The music industry is one of the darkest ones out there. I was in no way ready to be thrown into this arena at 19 years old. I am so grateful to my manager Papa Jon for believing in me and all the support he gave me for those years of pursuing my dream! I gained much experience and insight pursuing a singing career. Again, I believe everything happens for a reason. And through it all, I am thankful for music and the role that it has played throughout my life.

Another "breathe-in-and-out" moment, the pageant was over, and it was time to move on to the next chapter of my life. Moving on included a three-week vacation with my family and Clif. We were headed to the peaceful haven of the Smokey Mountains, to my grandparent's cabins in Northern Georgia. This was followed by my first trip back to Chicago with Clif to meet his family. From the moment I saw that beautiful skyline reflecting on the water of Lake Michigan it felt like home.

CHAPTER 7

A Fairytale Romance

Clifton's and my relationship progressed quickly. We were talking about marriage after only a few months. We both had been in serious relationships before and knew we had found "the one" with each other. His past consisted of a seven year stretch of on again off again with his high school girlfriend. My past included a broken engagement.

I was completely transparent with Clif and explained to him my background story that led to this crossroad in my life. I had lived in my parents' house my entire life except for a few months when I had stayed with a cousin. I have always loved my mom and dad, but we went through some tough years, like most do doing the teen years of trying to gain independence. My parents have often said I was spanked and grounded more than my brother and sister put together. For a stretch of time in my teen years, I was dealing with a lot of anger, and felt like nothing I did was ever good enough for them. The angrier I got the more I seemed to disappoint them. They say they were less strict with me than my siblings, but it did not feel like that to me. I often felt I was not allowed to make my own decisions about anything. Even though I have a strong personality, when it comes to authority figures, I still struggle to find my voice to this day. This is a likely product of my roots of trauma and abuse, I still deal with fear of failure, fear of letting authority figures down, and fear of losing their favor and love. This turns quickly to anger if I don't turn it over to Christ and focus on what He says about me.

At 20 years old I hit a wall. I was burning the candle at both ends between working full time, going to school full time, and trying to have a social life. I was stressed beyond words and often speeding home to make my 11 o'clock curfew. It was during a huge blow up with my dad about my room being a mess, that I packed my bags and left. I was honestly worried if I stayed, it would forever damage my relationship with my him. Their rules were established for my safety, but I couldn't see it that way. I was out from under their protection and quickly made choices that led to heartache. I was dealing with such turmoil during this phase of my life that I developed shingles in my eye. I desperately wanted to have my own voice and make my own decisions, but honestly didn't know how to. So, when I met a boy and fell in love, I knew it was my chance to do things my own way, which I did and then quickly regretted it.

Many wonder to this day why I got engaged the first time, only to call it off months later. Trust me, I had my reasons. I had been pressured into the engagement after regrettably allowing our relationship to go to a physical level that it should not have. Although I knew this man would make a wonderful husband, I also knew down inside he was not the one for me. I didn't want either of us to "settle" for anything less than God's best for our lives. I eventually felt like I was suffocating. So, I took one of the hardest steps I had up to that point in my life and ended the relationship. I clearly remember the night I called it off. As I drove away with him in my rear-view mirror, I felt immediate relief and a weight lifted off my shoulders. That confirmed I made the right decision. I was not panicking or drawn to turn around to try and fix it. I had peace in the midst of heartache. I faced a lot of judgment in the months that followed. I felt guilty over hurting him and his family and I know people who knew and loved us were confused. I stood up for what I felt was best. It was only a matter of months after the relationship ended that my accident happened. And even facing death did not sway me to return to a comfort zone and re-enter a relationship with him. It was confirmation again to me that I had made the right choice.

They say, "When you know, you just know," and that is spot on. When you meet the individual God has created for you, there is a peace that passes all understanding. You fit together with them perfectly. Like puzzle pieces created to match up, from how your hand fits into his, how his arms comfort you when you are scared, and your souls tie together in a way you never dreamed possible. I believe in dynamite love because I found it. That doesn't mean true love is perfect, it's far from perfect. But imperfections create a unique beauty if you allow yourself to see it that way.

When I was dating Clif, I had been a nanny for almost five years for a wonderful family. They had become a huge part of my life, and even played a role in our engagement and wedding day. Clif was quite the romantic and always doing small gestures to remind me of his love. During our courting phase, Clif made me numerous CD's and would hide love notes all over with the acronym "SHMILY" written on them which stood for "see how much I love you." I would find them after he would leave to go back to Chicago and my heart would smile. It was little things like these that captured my heart and made me feel prized and cherished.

When it came to the proposal, Clif had quite an elaborate set up. He arranged a scavenger hunt for me starting at my employer's home. He wrote a series of poems as clues to lead me to the next one. He also placed a single crimson rose on top of each clue. For the first clue, Clif had one of the children I was a nanny for draw me a beautiful butterfly picture with his acronym on it.

The day of the proposal I was expecting him for a visit but I wasn't expecting this. Early in the day he called me from a strange number and I asked, "Where are you calling me from?" I sensed his closeness! Clif responded, "From a pay phone, I forgot my phone this morning." Bless his heart, he had been in such a rush to get on the plane that morning that he left his cell phone in the car! I guess a woman's intuition is right, he was close and running around my hometown laying out the path for me to take to lead to his proposal! That day, he had also taken my dad to lunch to ask for my hand in marriage. My dad often tells the story of introducing Clif to someone they saw at the restaurant as "his future son in law" and "that was why they were there." Clif said it broke the ice and made for a fun lunch all around.

Back at my job, I found the drawn picture that told me to go to the car where the first poem was:

I am so excited to write this poem for you

And that you're reading it right now

I knew someday I would find you

I just didn't know when, where or how

God placed in my heart a long time ago

That my soul mate would one day be found

But who knew that only one look into your beautiful eyes would reveal it

Instead of me looking all around

That's right my dear, I'm telling you

From the bottom of my heart

That it's you my heart has always longed for

And I've known it from the start

However, this note is just the beginning

Of this fun little rhyme

I am ready to start my life with you

One that will stand the test of time

So, what I have planned tonight

You cannot do it alone
The next thing I want you to do
Is to carefully drive home
The reason for this is simple
This is where you started your life
I am so grateful for how your parents raised you
Because mine have prayed for a Godly wife
This drive to your house represents the beginning
A step you have taken with your family
Then your parents will give you the next clue...
How God had blessed this broken road
Which lead you straight to me!

This poem instructed me to go home where I found the second poem. My heart raced as I picked up the rose atop of each poem. With each clue, I paused and thanked the Lord for blessing me with a man who would take the time to do such a romantic gesture for me!

The second poem read:

So, the first stage of your journey is over
And you're ready to spread your wings and fly

But you need a partner for this endeavor

One who will help you sail into the sky

This next drive represents our adolescence

And our life's search to find true love

None of our past relationships were God's plan

But you must have been sent to me from up above

I'm so glad we didn't settle

For a lesser love than this

Because I knew you were someone special

From the very first time we kissed

So now my search is over

Because I have found my "one"

You are my soul mate, partner, and best friend

And together we have so much fun

So, by now you're probably asking

What's next for me to do?

Well now I want you to go to the place

Where God led me to you

I know that time stood still that day

As you stole my heart with a smile

In case you haven't guessed it yet

It's where I first walked you down the aisle!

Back to the sanctuary I went. I tried to catch my breath as I walked up the stairs to that same church that held some of the first memories we made together. My hand trembled as I reached out to the brass handle to open the heavy door. My heart fluttered and I caught my breath at the awe-inspiring sight I was taking in! Stunning red velvet rose petals all over the aisles, with candles dazzlingly leading the way to my future husband at the front of the church. I fought back tears as I walked nervously down the aisle knowing he was watching my every move. I looked in front of me and there he was, magnificent in a dark suit playing a guitar as he started to sing a Richard Marx song to me:

Whenever I'm weary from the battles that rage in my head

You make sense of madness when my sanity hangs by a thread

I lost my way but still you seem to understand

Now and forever I will be your man.

Sometimes I just hold you

Too caught up in me to see

I'm holding a fortune that heaven has given to me

I'll try to show you each and every way I can

Now and forever, I will be your man

Now I can rest my worries and always be sure
That I won't be alone anymore
If I'd only known you were there all the time
All this time
Until the day the ocean doesn't touch the sand
Now and forever, I will be your man
Now and forever, I will be your man.

I knew he meant every word, and as he placed his guitar beside him and got down on one knee, I couldn't believe I was so blessed to be living in this moment. Clif smiled up at me and with that sparkle in his beautiful blue eyes said, "Cassidy, I've waited for you my whole life. The moment I met you I knew you were the one God created for me. Will you do me the honor..." I interrupted his speech I was so thrilled and squealed "Yes! Yes! Yes!"

He started laughing at my animation and took me in his arms where we just stayed for several minutes, captivated in *our* moment, encompassed in *our* love and excitement for *our future.*

CHAPTER 8

Meet Me At The Alter

After that night Clif proposed, wedding bells were sounding in my every thought. We were planning on taking our time with the ceremony preparations, but the long-distance commute was getting harder on us every day. We longed to be with each other. When you're able see the love of your life only once a month, it's unbearable. So, plans soon sped up as we prepared for a spring wedding on the beach at sunset. It was a dream I'd had since I was a little girl, and Clif thought it was a tremendous idea as well. I figured what could make a ceremony more stunning than God's uniquely painted sunset as the backdrop? We started research-ing venues on the gulf side of Florida, and soon found the perfect spot.

Then came time to pick the date, and as it turned out, the availability for the hotel was March 19, 2006 – *exactly* one year to the day Clif walked me down the aisle the first time! Which means we would share the same anniversary as our wonderful friends who introduced us.

Our parents met each other for the first time at our beach themed engagement party in Florida. Thankfully, everyone hit it off and were supportive of our love. His parents Jerry and Lil were planning a second reception for us back in Chicago to celebrate with their family and friends that couldn't make the trip down for the wedding. They had also set up an engagement party for us in Chicago for me to meet everyone.

Lil threw the most elegant bridal shower at a beautiful restaurant. I felt very special. Everyone was so accepting of me at my shower and most generous with their gifts, even though some had never met me. Clif's sister Angela also helped with the shower. I was happy to have another sister and a friend close to my age when I made the move to Illinois. Clif's brother had purchased a condo and was renovating it during our engagement, and we decided we would rent it from him as our first place to live after we got married.

All the wedding arrangements were coming along without a hitch, and I couldn't have been more eager to start this new chapter of my life marrying the man of my dreams! My mom and I came up with several creative ways to cut costs for my wedding budget, making the centerpieces and floral arrangements ourselves.

Clif and I took one dance lesson so he could learn some basic steps, and from that I choreographed our first dance complete with a couple lifts. We had picked "Now and Forever" the song he sang when he proposed to me. We also put together a list of wonderful worship and love songs for our ceremony. One of them I wrote and recorded myself after meeting and falling in love with Clif. Every precious detail of our wedding had significant meaning. It was difficult at times making our wedding arrangements while living so far apart. I wanted Clif to be as involved as he could be every step of the way.

It took many hours of preparation and calls to detail, but it was worth it. One of our main goals was to have our wedding be a witness of God's love and what he had done in each of our lives. We knew it would be held on a public beach and wanted it to share the gospel to anyone passing by.

Our day came quickly! I couldn't believe how much of a whirlwind romance it truly was. To our dismay, we learned just weeks before the wedding that they double-booked our date with another client, so I was trying not to stress over this as the wedding day approached.

Thankfully we got a discount on the reception hall and some additional accommodations due to the hotel's error. The Lord promises to work all things together for our good! The weather in Florida is very unpredictable in March, but our prayers paid off. The days before and after our day were frigid, but it warmed up just for our wedding. The day we rehearsed on the beach with our closest family and friends, I looked around in amazement that I would be a wife in less than 24 hours.

My sister, who is a fabulous photographer, brought her camera and captured some breathtaking pictures of Clif and me on the beach with the sunset after our rehearsal. To this day, they are some of my favorite photos of us!

March 19, 2006, started out with a bang—literally since the hotel was under construction and the power kept going out in our rooms as we tried to get ready for the ceremony. We ended up having to move rooms three times. I had some wonderful friends present who made the day special in numerous ways. My childhood best friend Jaime was there to hold my hand through the stress of the day, and she did my hair and makeup for the ceremony. Many of my bridesmaids helped in any way possible to help the day go off as planned. Some of my wonderful Aunts were there as well decorating, fixing, and offering a hand to help wherever they could. My mom was the best coordinator, designer, friend, encourager, organizer, arranger, and prayer warrior you could ask for! She put so much love into making everything intricately special. Every detail was planned with love.

Clif and I chose to do a special first look together before the ceremony. It was overwhelming to see the love in his eyes. We also took time to pray together before the ceremony started. The other wedding ended in just the nick of time and it was time to walk down the aisle. "Wonderful Merciful Savior", by Selah played as I walked onto the beach, barefoot at sunset, holding my daddy's arm. I took in my surroundings, and it seemed too good to be true. A gentle breeze blowing in the palm trees, the most gorgeous hues of orange and pink painted across the sky, my loved one's encircled in the bright glowing tiki torches, and my handsome groom awaiting me with that irresistible dimple grin.

What a gift and tribute it was to the both of us that we had friends come from all over the country to share in our special day. Even my friend Evalina, a foreign exchange student who lived with us my senior year of high school, came all the way from Germany! Clif's dad said it was a testament to what great friends we had been for these individuals to come all this way. What an honor. It was also a blessing to have Clif's dad sing and play guitar for our ceremony. He was the first to welcome me to the family, which meant a lot to me.

We were surrounded by loved ones who gave their blessings as we made our vows and started our lives together. The ceremony was full of laughter, dancing, and delicious food. Our wedding cake was cheesecake which is my absolute favorite. That night we stayed in a beautiful penthouse suite overlooking the beautiful ocean. My wedding was all I hoped for and more. And they lived happily ever...

CHAPTER 9

The Nightmare Begins

I was very busy during those six months of preparation before the wedding. Working full time, going to school at night, planning an out-of-town wedding, and packing up my entire life to move across the country. I was so caught up in the busyness of everything and the "high" of being in love, that I never took the time to prepare myself mentally and emotionally for the move away from everything I'd ever known. The undealt with emotional turmoil from my accident was brewing inside, on top of my unprocessed childhood wounding. I was a ticking emotional time bomb just waiting for someone to light the fuse.

Living in small-town Ocala, Florida, was all I had ever known. It was charming, but boy was I in for culture shock moving to Chicago! People and "life" in general are completely different in the North. To me, southern individuals seem to be more laid back and family-centered while up North they tend to be more fast-paced and career driven. Often people get married and start a family right out of high school where I came from. Many individuals I met in Chicago thought I was too young to be getting married at 22, and I am still getting used to the bluntness of other's opinions–whether you ask for it or not! I went from being a big fish in the pond of Ocala, to a guppy in the large sea of Chicago. I knew nothing and no one, and quickly fell into depression and longed for home. I missed my family and friends so much. I desperately clung to Clif and placed him as my top priority, losing myself in being his wife. I was wrong to essentially idolize him trying to be fulfilled through him. That was an unrealistic expectation for both of us.

Then the nightmares started. Shortly after I moved, full blown memories resurfaced of sexual abuse at a very young age. Horrific memories of blankets silencing me, rug burns on my back, bleeding in the bathtub, not knowing how to say "no" time and time again. I was still healing from my brain injury, not only physically but emotionally, and now memories I had suppressed were creating massive inner turmoil. Unexpectedly, the pain of what I had endured all those years ago felt raw and real and present.

Clif and I found ourselves facing conflict from the

very beginning of our marriage with family issues and clashing personalities. It is hard to merge two lives together as one in any circumstance but add in the complexity of brain injury and severe physical trauma, and things get messy and volatile pretty quickly. I was lonely, highly emotional, and desperate to figure out what home was in this new chapter of my life. I can honestly say I really had no clue where to begin. I was losing what little was left of myself. I was spiraling in inner turmoil.

On top of everything, my brother-in-law was still finishing the renovations on the condo which meant we were living in an unfinished condo with no kitchen sink, counter tops, or dishwasher. I would wash dishes in the tub or laundry sink in the community room. Cooking was also difficult with nowhere to put anything. In an emotional moment, I found myself at the pet store clinging to a puppy which brought me comfort. So, I bought it and brought home even though the condo we lived in did not allow dogs. This was a foolish decision on my end. Needless to say, it strained my relationship with Clif and his brother, our landlord. We were asked to move out on very short notice. We looked desperately to find another place but with no fast luck, we were forced to move in with Clif's parents. Yes, we were grateful for their generosity, but it naturally put *another* strain on our marriage as newlyweds living at home with parents, and our puppy.

While Clif went to work, I felt awkward not being in my own home. Due to my homesickness, and all the sexual abuse memories resurfacing, I had become easily triggered emotionally, and responded to others in an elevated state. Understandably, Clif's family didn't know what I was dealing with inside, so my broken, touchy behavior was met with criticism and disapproval from them. My mom always told me, "Blood is thicker than water." I was the outsider and everything I did wrong was magnified. Worse, I couldn't understand why I struggled to control these outbursts. In my heart I was a genuine and loving woman but my actions portrayed something different simply because so much was unhealed inside. The reality was, at times I was immersed in dysfunction and strife unlike anything I had never known. It felt like chaos surrounded me and I found myself anxious about every family gathering. I was worrying about what would happen next, or what would be said about me behind closed doors. I was seeing things through the eyes of offense and bracing myself for the next backlash. I saw what I was looking for and read into things through the filter of my brokenness. Foolishly, I expected Clif to fill my voids, stand up for me, and protect me. He did the best he could, but he was learning to navigate this un-charted territory and rough waters of a new marriage with a sensitive bride. He had taught himself to avoid conflict in his survival mode so when I got emotionally hot, he would emotionally disappear. This came across to me as emotional abandonment which added fodder to the fire. I fell further into depression and insecurity. I needed to turn to God instead of relying solely on Clif to be my healer. It wasn't Clif's role to make me happy and secure. In my hurt I deified him and was let down. Only Christ can heal our brokenness. Only Christ can fulfill the longings of our hearts and make us whole.

No one else is responsible for *your* happiness but you. Only God can define your worth, fill those voids, and leave you lacking in nothing. Regardless of what you may be going through today, **you** have the abil-ity to turn to Him and find rest for your weary soul. He alone is the lifter of your head. Every family has issues. Each person must be willing to do the work it takes to make a relationship strong. In marriage, you are coming together to create something new. But you must be willing to take the time to talk and listen to each other, even when you don't agree. This isn't easy because everyone has different communication styles. The most important thing is to come together in love, grace, and respect. We need to allow the other person to share where they are coming from, without inter-rupting, and truly hear them. Because we are imper-fect people, living in an imperfect world, we all expe-rience pain in life. And we all make mistakes and hurt others at times, even if unintentional. We must be willing to admit where we have fallen short and were wrong. In a conflict neither side is completely guilty, or completely innocent. Mending and healing isn't about determining who is right or wrong, it's about forgiveness and determining how to move forward. It takes two people to argue. And it takes two people to reconcile. But if the other individual refuses to com-municate or try and work through it, what do you do? Forgive and pray for them. If someone else accuses you of things you never did and spreads lies about your character, what do you do? Forgive and pray for them. This is true for *any* relationship. It is so painful when an individual is poisoning others against you, but you have to trust that the Lord will bring out the truth and defend you.

I've had to ask the Lord to help me put the law of kindness on my tongue many times with my defensive responses. I have been guilty of venting my frustra-tions to others when aggravations arise, and I should have taken the matter to the Lord instead. It is neces-sary that we walk in the fruit of the spirit as Christ followers. We are distinguished from unbelievers in that we are gifted by the Holy Spirit to enable us to bear fruit.

> *"The fruit of the spirit is love, joy, peace, patience, kindness, generosity, faithfulness, gentleness, self-control; against such things there is no law."*
>
> **GALATIANS 5: 22-23 NIV**

We must be willing to forgive over and over again as Christ has forgiven us, even if the other individual never asks for forgiveness. I recently heard a message that shared, "A person who cannot forgive has forgotten what they have been forgiven of." The Bible warns us that holding onto offense and unforgiveness is like drinking poison from our own cup. Sadly, generational curses, spiritual strife, and contention play a huge role in dividing families. I feel it is crucial to mention that I believe that the enemy has been at work here, and it's important not to place blame on any one individual. Also, grace needs to be given when dealing with mental illness and past wounds.

> *"For we do not wrestle against flesh and blood, but against the rulers, against the authorities, against the cosmic powers over this present*

darkness, against the spiritual forces of evil in the heavenly places."

EPHESIANS 6:12 ESV

It has been heartbreaking to witness, and even harder to not fall into the unhealthy patterns of contention. Negativity and criticism can rub off on you easily. It is crucial to seek the Lord daily so that we are not deceived by the schemes and plans of the enemy in our lives. Offense obscures personal views. It often changes perceptions, and realities of situations. We must not hold onto offense! We must forgive quickly and completely.

I also had to learn that my value does not decrease based on someone's inability to see my worth. I am growing and learning to not let what others think of me dictate who I am, or the choices I make. Even if these individuals are relatives. Allowing other's opinions in, can lead us to losing our self-worth and self-esteem, and sometimes even our self-respect. This can lead us astray into thinking we are bound for failure if we are not careful in guarding our hearts. It doesn't have to be this way. I am *still* striving to love with Christ's love and have healthier boundaries in many of my relationships. And life brings plenty of growing opportunities.

Valuing our self-worth is an important part of our journey towards happiness, confidence, success, and life satisfaction. Life is full of pain and disappointments, but when we are feeling defeated, it should never keep us from reaching for our highest potential or cause us to question our self-worth.

It is also crucial to accept the fact that you can't control what others do to you, you can only control how you respond. Our spiritual maturity is measured by our recovery time. The more mature we are in Christ, the faster we will let go of offense and forgive. We lose when we try to defend ourselves against false accusations. God will always defend us better than we can defend ourselves.

"The Lord will fight for you and you shall hold your peace you only need to be still."

EXODUS 14:14 NIV

There are some people in life, no matter how hard you try, they will dislike you. Think about this, God who has never sinned or done anything wrong has people who hate Him just because. My two strongest love languages are gift giving and words of affirmation. What I've learned over the years, is that we cannot expect others to love or receive love the same way we do. And the more we try to force a relationship, the worse it gets. We must let go and trust the Lord. We must wait on his timing and not try to make our own agenda happen.

Did you know that in Peter 2:17a the Lord instructs us to honor **everyone**? God calls us to honor all men for the simple fact they are His creation.

"Outdo one another in showing honor."

ROMANS 12:10B ESV

I had to repent for talking about and thinking ill-will of those who had hurt and betrayed me. If we dishonor others, we open a door of retaliation in our lives. We can't choose our family members, but we can choose to bloom through rejection and betrayal. Even if a situation seems hopeless, Luke 1:37 reminds us, "Nothing is impossible with God." He can work on every heart involved.

If you are weary from difficult relationships in your life, I want to encourage you to hold strong to the promises of His Word. Through it all, continue to show Christ's love and live at peace as much as it is in your power to do so. When someone judges you, remember that pain, and be careful not to judge and criticize others in return. You can continue to love with Christ's love. And it is important to pray for those who have hurt you and bless those who persecute you. Don't allow yourself to get stuck in a rut of trying to bring about breakthrough in your own ways. Some relationships are for a reason, some for a season, and some for a lifetime. Seek the Lord, it may be time to accept what you cannot change and move on.

CHAPTER 10

Love Is A Choice

Clif and I were two broken individuals trying to merge our lives together. We often say we dated after we got married, and there is a lot of truth to this. It takes a long time to truly know a person, and we got to know each other as the years progressed, and we worked hard at molding our lives together as one. I soon found out Clif dealt with anxiety too. He felt stuck in the middle between his new wife and his family. When the stress levels would rise, Clif returned to a destructive habit that he thought he had mastered long ago. Pornography. Clif had been exposed at a very young age and the enemy took a foothold.

The enemy preys on young boys because he knows how easy it is to entrap them. He knows they are supposed to be the head of their future households. Pornography is rampant in our society today. Everywhere you turn there is soft porn attacking our men's minds and continually tempting them with lust. The enemy knows that a sexual addiction is stronger than even a heroin addiction. Yes, it's true. It's so deceitful because it roots itself deep inside the individual, convincing them they are doing nothing wrong in their private moments of indulging their sin. Because it involves no one "in the flesh," individuals with a porn addiction often convince themselves they are not hurting anyone. But the damage it does to their psyche and perception of what an intimate relationship should look like is untold. Men are manipulated by our society convincing them it's not really cheating, but it is. Just like most sin, it often has a root of pride.

Jesus said in Matthew 5:28, "If a man so much as looks at a woman with lust in his heart he has already committed adultery."

There are many books that share extensive research on the detriments of pornography. It starts with a second look, such as a lingerie ad, then a lustful thought, which leads to wanting more to get that thrill, that dopamine hit. Objectifying body parts becomes jumbled in the tangled web of lust. The slippery slope of porn often leads to affairs, and sometimes even rape or murder. Ted Bundy, and many others, have admitted that their issues started with pornography. Like any addiction, you keep craving *more*, until you reach the point where the pornography only goes so far. Ted Bundy in his final interview before his execution stated:

"I've lived in prison for a long time now, and I've met a lot of men who were motivated to commit violence. Without exception, every one of them was deeply involved in pornography–deeply consumed by the addiction."

Sadly this is not an issue only men struggle with. Now many young girls (almost 50%) are also becoming addicted as they are assaulted with online images, seeking to learn what it means to "be a woman" and capture a man's attention. There is much danger from the digital age we live in.

There are many secular statistics on the detriment of pornography as well, on both individuals and in relationships. In fact, it has been listed as public health risk! It not only wreaks havoc on souls, now there are studies that prove the damaging effects on minds and bodies as well. Even governmental officials have stated that as pornography becomes more prolific and mainstream, our society becomes more desensitized and violent. It has led to increased degradation of women, rise in sexual violence, advancement in human trafficking, and rise in domestic violence. It is not just detrimental to those with addictive traits, porn's negativity can affect anyone, and impacts relationships in a number of ways. Pornography effects mental health as well, and studies show increases in depression. It also decreases life satisfaction. It is a false sense of reality, and comparison is a thief of joy.

There is much truth in the saying:

Be careful what you think, thoughts become words.

Be careful what you say, words turn into actions.

Be careful of your actions, actions become your habits.

Be careful of your habits, because they become your life!

Our eyes and ears are the gateways to our souls. We must guard our hearts and minds.

Your life is shaped by your thoughts.

"Keep your heart with all vigilance, for from it flows the springs of life."

PROVERBS 4:23 ESV

I was very young and naive, thinking that because my husband was the love of my life, he would have never looked at anything like pornography or visited places like strip clubs. The topic had come up in our pre-marital counseling, but Clif had quickly denied anything ever happening because he felt it had been dealt with and didn't want to worry me, not to mention the shame the enemy heaps on. It's a deep-rooted addiction that can raise its ugly head at any moment. Like all addictions, it gives you a false sense of assurance that you can control it at any time. If you are dealing with any hidden sin in your life, it is crucial you bring it to light, confess it, and get accountability. Clif often quotes, "Whatever you can't talk about has power over you."

As newlyweds, we had fallen into unhealthy patterns in our marriage, and when tension arose, Clif felt anxiety and fell back into sinful addictions to escape. I, on the other hand, turned to food. I quickly put on weight and was upset with myself in many areas.

I still remember the first time I found out about his addiction. Enraged devastation is putting it "lightly." Men have no idea what they do to the women in their lives by desiring someone else. Remember my "easily triggered" emotional state? Well, this certainly triggered it. I responded horribly in rage. I was not a safe place for Clif to come to, or even approach this topic. I needed help to sort through my anger. Clif was the first man I had opened my entire heart to. I had shared everything there was to know about me with him, every dark secret. I was so emotionally vulnerable to him that this crushed me almost to the point of no repair. I had unknowingly put him in a place in my life that the Lord alone should have been all along.

After I found out, I packed my bags to leave, terrified that I didn't know this man I had shared my life with at all. My parents told me over the phone, "You've made vows with him for better or worse." By the grace of God, thankfully, I listened and stayed. Several months would go by and everything was fine, then another slip up would come. My trust was shattered not only in him, but in love itself. I felt like I was losing my mind with the mental games coming up from his addiction.

All the emotions and wounds of me being sexually abused resurfaced every time the sexual sin happened in his secret life. I am thankful now looking back at how much the Lord cared about Clif, myself, and our marriage to bring these issues into the light. At the time, it was hard to see it that way. I was furious that he never came to me with "slip ups" but that I had to discover them myself every single time. I was always on high alert and I felt he wasn't truly sorry because he had never brought it into the light on his own.

I finally had to learn that I could not be Clif's or anyone else's Holy Spirit. This was how the enemy was entrapping me with bitterness, resentment, and disrespect towards my husband. Thankfully, I sought counsel.

"For waging war you need guidance, and for victory many advisors."

PROVERBS 24:6 NIV

Take it from me, it is crucial during your lowest valleys to get counsel from a godly source. Good Christian counsel will always encourage you to forgive and find freedom. If you are not careful, you can fall into sin yourself very quickly and ruin your marriage. When we are vulnerable, the enemy often attacks. We must not isolate.

Our healing journey was long, and felt like one step forward, and two steps back. I couldn't understand how Clif could do this to me. Did he not love me at all? My heart physically hurt and I experienced my first panic attack, unable to breathe. I was sickened and repulsed by him, yet also desperate for his love and simpler times. I wanted to keep him close to me. All the counselors and resources I read kept reassuring me that it had nothing to do with me. I struggled to accept that truth. I felt worthless, unattractive, and like a failure at the one thing that mattered the most to me—being a great wife.

In seeking the Lord and doing much research on the topic, I found that instead of focusing on Clif's sin, I needed to deal with my *own* sin. Like my friend Val often says, "We can't put a bow on our sin." My anger and resentment were just as much of a sin as what Clif was doing. As I prayed and surrendered all to the Lord, He helped me see Clif as my brother in Christ with his struggles and gave me compassion towards him.

In today's world, men have it tough to walk in integrity. It takes much courage to stand up against the things the enemy throws in their paths. They are slammed with temptation every day with magazine covers at the checkout lines, on billboards as they drive down the street, on television commercials, sexually-driven shows, and pop-up ads on YouTube and social media. It in their faces everywhere! Pornography is a destructive addiction for each one involved and more. It desensitizes men and women and renders them incapable of true intimacy. We need to pray for the men in our lives with fervent unrelenting prayers.

"For everything in the world—the lust of the flesh, the lust of the eyes, and the pride of life—comes not from the Father but from the world."

1 JOHN 2:16

We also need to remember to dress modestly and raise virtuous daughters who know their true beauty comes from inside and not from their bodies.

"I also want the women to dress modestly,
with decency and propriety, adorning themselves,
not with elaborate hairstyles or gold pearls
or expensive clothes."

1 TIMOTHY 2:9 NIV

Any attention we gain from our looks is not fulfilling for long, and it's a slippery dangerous slope. **I am not saying women are responsible for men choosing to lust**, but we do have responsibility to present ourselves as Christ's ambassadors.

"Do you know that your bodies are temples
of the Holy Spirit, who is in you, whom you have
received from God? You are not your own.
You were bought with a price. Therefore, honor God
with your bodies."

1 CORINTHIANS 6:19-20 NIV

We need to be careful not to judge men in their struggles as well. And we need to be cautious to not act out in ways that can cause sin. Each of us will be held accountable for *everything* we say and do.

*"Therefore let us stop passing judgment on one
another. Instead, make up your mind not to put any
stumbling block or obstacle in the way of a brother
or sister."*

ROMANS 14:13 NIV

I am here to offer you hope in your darkest hour.
Anything and everything, and I mean *everything*, can
be forgiven. No matter how deep the pain or betrayal
goes, you *can* forgive with the help of Christ.

We must forgive. Every single time. Even if they
never ask for our forgiveness, we *must* forgive all the
things that have been done to us. And we can with the
help of the Lord!

I strongly urge you on this quest of forgiveness because I've walked both sides, and my faith was put
through the fire when a new level of betrayal arose.

CHAPTER 11

Ready, Set, Grow

Our marriage had been through much, and without even trying, we found ourselves pregnant. Excited about this next chapter, with hopes of it bringing us closer together, we set off for our first ultrasound. My cousin Sarah had moved up to Chicago after marrying one of Clif's friends. It was such a blessing to have her there with me. What a shock to hear, "Surprise! It's twins!"

Within a week I was sick. And by sick, I mean nauseous and vomiting every day and night with no relief no matter what I tried. It felt like a never ending bout of the stomach bug. I was tested and found out I had a rare condition called hyperemesis gravidarum. Less than 3% of pregnant women get this, and *lucky me*, I was one of them. I could not keep anything down and got to the point of not being able to stand anymore, so we went to the hospital for IVs. Another ultrasound showed the babies were okay. In fact, we had four ultrasounds all confirming we were having twins. It wasn't until we were sent to Maternal Fetal Medicine Specialist (a high-risk pregnancy facility often for multiples) that we discovered...they were actually triplets!

I remember the day well. I was sick as could be and trying not to throw up during my exam. The nurse turned to me and asked me who diagnosed me having twins. I thought, Oh maybe they got it wrong and there is just one baby. Um, nope, there were three distinct babies on the ultrasound machine! I almost fainted and immediately started to cry telling the nurse, "But my mom is in Florida! How can I do this without her?" Clif just kept saying he was sorry over and over. To say we were in shock was an understatement. It's the only ultrasound picture I have of the three of them together. There they were—one, two, three miracles bouncing around in my womb.

I had been working as a theater instructor and vocal coach and was not able to continue much longer. I also had become the worship leader at Pastor Mike's church who had moved up from Ocala. Clif and I served in this ministry for four years and we went through a lot, and we learned much. When you are behind the scenes in ministry you see it all. The good, the bad, and the ugly. We've also been a part of a couple different church plants that will grow your servant's heart real quick like! I was thankful for the growing season in ministry, but ready to take a backseat and grow some healthy babies, which was my new number one priority.

I had several doctors' appointments to keep up with as well. It was a whirlwind to prepare for three babies on the way. I ended up losing 22 pounds as those three little ones were sucking the life out of me. Like clock-work, they would wake me up every morning at 5:00 A.M. Clif would make me a protein shake to drink and they would all go back to sleep. I wish I would've had a smart phone during my pregnancy to capture my stomach and the babies' movements. When one would roll over, they all would roll over. And anytime I put something on top of my belly they would kick it off as to tell me "Mom, there's no more room!" Having a multiples pregnancy is not for the faint of heart. I was so traumatized from all the needles from my brain in-jury that I was nervous for what was to come. But af-ter having to get blood work done every other week, I quickly got over that fear.

I developed Pupps which is an extremely irritating hive-like rash during my pregnancy. It is common when carrying multiples. It covered my stomach and legs. I also developed dangerously high blood pressure and my resting heart rate was in the 120s. I had to take it as easy as possible to keep from going into preterm labor.

We had to find a new car, so we took three car seats and a triplet stroller with us to each dealership to try and find a vehicle that would be conducive. We had to find a new home because our tiny town home wouldn't work, and we needed something preferably without stairs. We had to find a new OBGYN who specialized in multiples. We had to find a hospital with a level three NICU. And we had to get three of everything for our precious little ones on the way. It was a blessing to go shopping at garage sales and when the sellers would find out we were carrying triplets, they often threw in baby items for free. Also, we met some of our future closest friends when we went to their sale, then low and behold, years later we met again at a new church! Our daughters are now growing up as close friends and it blesses my heart how the Lord strategically places individuals in our paths.

We soon found out it was three girls! A couple of newspapers featured a story on my miraculous healing from my accident to then go on and conceive natural triplets. Soon after the articles ran, we were featured on a local television news channel on a morning show in Chicago. They had us on the show again once the girls were born.

We were blessed with three incredible baby showers. And we felt loved and supported in many ways. Even strangers were sending us hand-me-down clothes and items to help.

My goal was to make it to 35 weeks which is full term for triplets. I was sent into labor and delivery 17 times due to high blood pressure and contractions. On the early morning hours of August 29, 2010, I knew something was different. Sure enough, my body had gone into pre-eclampsia, and it was time for the girls to come at 34 weeks and 5 days. We grabbed a measuring tape out of Clif's work truck before we headed off to the hospital and I measured 55 inches around on the day of delivery! Think about it, almost as wide as I was tall.

We were led through the NICU before delivery to prepare us for what was to come with possible incubation, wires, monitors, tubes, and monitoring machines. We had also been warned due to them being preemies they probably wouldn't be strong enough to cry. What a relief that each of them did! I was in the operating room when they brought Clif back and he said he literally saw my organs out on the table. There were so many individuals in the operating room for that C-section: a cardiologist in case my heart gave out, two of my OBGYN doctors, an anesthesiologist, three NICU doctors with two nurses for each baby, and nurses for me.

Each girl came out weighing around four-pounds which is great for a preemie and multiple! And they all came out with same blood type and cute little cowlick on the back of their heads. We decided to have DNA testing done and found out our miracle babies were in fact, identical triplets!

Cadence Lily was named after Clif's mom Lillian. Cailynn Juliet was named after my mom's middle name and my great grandmother. Chloe Glo was named after my middle name and my aunt Glo and grandmother Gloria. I believe my daughters have an incredible call on their lives! And I know they are one of the biggest reasons my life was spared all those years ago.

The hardest part of the delivery was when it took almost an hour for them to put my organs back in place, then having them pressing on my stomach to get all the air out. If I could do it all over again, I would choose to be put under. I ended up having post-eclampsia which is a rare dangerous condition that can cause seizures or stroke. I also ran a fever shortly after delivery for a few days. A blessing that came from this was that I was able to stay in the hospital, close to the girls. I was there for ten days being monitored. They were doing well, all things considered, but would need to stay in the hospital for a bit. Cailynn and Cadence were able to come home first after being in the NICU for two weeks. Our little Chloe had to stay for a month due to having bradycardia and needed to come home with a heart monitor for about four additional months. It was so hard for my momma heart to leave her behind to take the other two home. I went back every day to spend time with her and pray over her. Chloe would not be left behind. She became the first to roll over, sit up, crawl and walk. Chloe is a warrior.

My mom and dad came up to help for a month after the girls were born, and it is some of the most treasured memories I have with them. Clif's parents also were a huge help with the girls, and to this day Lil comes one day a week to help me with homeschooling and around the house. Jerry wrote a song for each of the girls on his guitar that he sings for them often. All three girls have grown into healthy, happy, beautiful girls. They have been an absolute joy to watch grow and have the most unique beautiful bond together. What an incredible honor the Lord chose me to be their mom and entrusted them into my care. I have so many things to divulge on raising triplets. I have actually written a moms-of-multiples book to share helpful things I learned.

Life was beautiful chaos, and we found ourselves in survival mode. The home that we had rented before the girls were born came with many challenges and an impossible landlord. We had more than nine roof leaks he refused to fix. The was an actual small tree growing out of part of the roof. We had mice infestation and hornets' nest in our walls coming in through the holes in the bricks. We had black mold starting to grow, and even mushrooms coming up in our kitchen. We sought legal advice after our daughters started to develop rashes and my asthma was being affected.

We tried to meet with the lessor on numerous occasions, and eventually had to move out under duress. The landlord then came after us with a lawsuit. It was a nightmare. During this same time the market went south due to the great recession, and we couldn't sell our town home. So, we had to continue to rent other homes and eventually short sell the town house. This kept us from being able to buy a home for four years. The new house we rented after the nightmare landlord, was fully furnished so we decided to store all our furniture in the basement. Within hours after moving our items in, we were notified that the fridge had flooded, and all of our items had been saturated. Challenge after challenge seemed to come our way. Clif was called to a deposition with the lawsuit regarding our previous rental. The lawyer had caught the landlord in many instances of double speak and overt lying about the circumstances of the lease in question, which elevated the line of questioning and responses between the lawyer and the landlord. Since things were so heated, the landlord's lawyer asked for a ten-minute break from the deposition. Clif left the deposition room to head to the lobby bathroom and when he returned the landlord had a massive heart attack right in front of him and died in the middle of the lobby. What a tragic situation all around.

We settled into the new rental house with the girls. Thankfully we had renter's insurance before moving in, and the insurance adjuster was an old acquaintance of Clif who gave us a favored amount to use towards future furniture. The wife of the landlord dropped the lawsuit and gave us back our security deposit. I started being asked to speak at some women's conferences and events and was enjoying being back at singing on the worship team.

It was during this time the Lord had laid on my heart to fast. He gave me the number seven, so I automatically thought that meant I would fast for seven days. On November 7, 2012, I was sitting down to prepare notes for an upcoming event I was speaking at when somehow, I opened up Clif's email on my computer. I was very confused thinking it was my inbox. I did not recognize a name on messages going back and forth, so I opened them to discover Clif was involved with another woman from his college years. My world shattered. I was in shock and disbelief as I looked through the messages. We had been in therapy for years. He had gone to recovery, accountability, and addiction support groups for help. We had gone to marriage conferences and made it through numerous self-help books together and on our own. How could this be happening? Surely this wasn't real. I pulled up our cell phone bill online, and there staring me in the face was more proof of hours of phone calls. I crumbled to the floor in our bedroom. I had a sitter over to help that day so I could prepare for the conference I was soon speaking at. I physically had to leave the house so the girls wouldn't see me falling apart. I felt like I couldn't breathe. I went and sat in the parking lot of a nearby park and cried like I never had before. Thank the Lord I had been fasting, praying, and spending time in the

Word. Otherwise, I don't think I would have been able to handle it. I screamed and wailed to the Lord, and He wrapped His loving arms around me when I felt I could not go on to face another day. Thankfully I had the common sense to pick up the phone and reach out for help. I couldn't do this alone. Not this level of betrayal and heartbreak.

My cousin Sarah dropped everything to come over and stay with me and help with the girls. I'm thankful she is not only family, but one of my closest friends as well. She was there when I needed someone to just sit there with me. She didn't try and tell me what to do, she didn't try and fix the problem, she just comforted and helped however she could, and that was exactly what I needed at that time.

Clif and I entered a time of separation, and I ended up heading to Florida with the girls to stay with my family during this very difficult season of growth in my life. During this time, I worked through many things personally, and my relationship with my parents grew to something beautiful. It was a switchover to an adult-to-adult relationship with them. I honestly don't know how I could have made it through these trials without my mom and dad. They inspired me, encouraged me, and challenged me in my growth with the Lord. They also challenged me in my prayer life, forgiveness, and love for Clif.

I was *determined* to grow. I would bloom regardless of the storm's life was throwing my way. God held me in the palm of his hand. He spoke to me very clearly to *stay* with Clif.

> *"What God has joined together,*
> *let no one separate."*
>
> **MARK 10:9 NIV**

My husband's testimony is life changing! I am so grateful we have faced what we have in our marriage, because it has helped us both grow individually in the Lord and strengthened our marriage in significant ways. I have been so impacted by what the Lord has done in my husband's life, so I have asked him to take a couple pages here to share part of his story on the road of redemption.

CHAPTER 12

It's A Slow Fade: *Clif Tells His Story*

"So I hated life, because the work that is done under the sun was grievous to me. All of it is mean-ingless, a chasing after the wind."

ECCLESIASTES 2:17-18 NIV

How is it that a man, who by many accounts was con-sidered one of the wisest and most knowledgeable men in the annals of recorded history could fall away from God and lose everything in the process?

Solomon started out with a contrite heart in full de-votion to the Lord. However, he allowed his love for material things and great accomplishments as a build-er to slowly move him away from a desire to please the Lord to a desire for the accolades and praises of men. He lived for the "atta boy" like many of us today living for our promotions, likes and shares. He lived for the pleasure he received from 700 wives and 300 concu-bines-and yet he was never fulfilled. Never satisfied. I suppose that's what he realizes when seven times in

Ecclesiastes he gives the analogy of chasing the wind. The wind is not something that can be caught. It's the perfect depiction for anything we go after in this world. If you could catch it, you would not feel like you had anything once you did. Always striving for more. Always needing it. Yet never fulfilled.

And so is where my journey begins...

I learned from an early age that many times, perception is reality. In my mind, what people "thought" of you was of high importance. I was always very concerned with what other people's impression was of me. Whether I was highly regarded or not, and whether I was someone that they wanted to be around. I was able to switch it on and off whenever I needed to be a particular way, with a particular person or group, to gain what I perceived as their approval.

This mindset was coupled with an upbringing that saw my older brother "pave the way" by getting into trouble at a fast clip. That nearly daily occurrence made me realize that I needed to be a certain way, act a certain way, and not ever allow myself to reveal who I *really* was for fear of repercussion from either my peers or my parents. I learned to wear a mask. It wasn't that anything had happened to me. I was just fine avoiding the "what ifs." I was just fine projecting an image of myself for others around me to see, and at the same time, not wanting to disappoint those closest to me.

The thing about wearing a mask is that you can never talk about what is REALLY going on. So, when harmful things come up, when the important conversations need to be had, mask wearers shy away from allowing ourselves to be vulnerable.

I may not have been wearing the "mask" at the age of eight when I was first exposed to pornography, but I did inherently know it was wrong. In fact, when I was first presented with the opportunity to watch it with a neighbor two years older than me, I resisted. Resisted to the point that he basically had to physically force me to watch it. I didn't want to. The strange part about this situation is that even though I can remember being initially repulsed by it, within maybe 20-30 minutes I was asking to watch it again...JUST THAT QUICK! The devil was laying the initial groundwork that would become a reoccurring theme later in my life. Even though I have no other clear remembrances of seeing anything at any other time, we subsequently moved away just over two years later, a hook was placed in my soul.

It wasn't until several years later that I was out on a

church youth outing, ironically enough, at a restaurant in downtown Chicago, when a group of the boys went to the bathroom and we were jokingly playing with a dispenser that was in there. As we pulled on the various knobs, to our surprise, different items began to drop including what I would later come to find out were condoms. We were laughing and having a good time with what we thought was good fortune until we became worried about getting in trouble. So, we hurriedly put the items in our pockets and got out of there before anyone saw that we were getting free stuff out of this vending machine.

After getting home with my "treasures" the curiosity of what I found would ultimately lead me down the path into masturbation and pornography which would carry on for years to follow.

It's no coincidence that Peter uses this analogy. If you have ever watched videos of lions hunting in Africa, they are strategic, and they are tactical. The don't go after the biggest and strongest. They go after the young, the sick, or the injured. The first thing that they do is zero in on a specific target. Then, they separate that target from the rest of the herd. This is why wearing a mask to hide your real self from the outside world is so dangerous. It causes isolation. Isolation causes us to be vulnerable to attacks from the enemy. As men, we are not meant to go at life alone. And yet, there are more lonely men today than at any point in recent history. We are setting ourselves up for failure!

Had I not been wearing a mask in my teenage years, and had I not cared about what others thought of me, I could have probably gotten through the refinement of this trial with a lot less future heartache. Instead, I carried on with my usual "everything was fine." Or so I thought.

It was also during this time that I started to excel in baseball. By my senior year of high school, I was garnering numerous accolades including First Team All-State, Male Athlete of The Year in my high school, and Player of The Year in two local newspapers among others. I received multiple Division 1 college offers and I began flying all over the country with my teams. With this new notoriety I always felt like I had to be everything to everyone. There were times that I was on local television. There were instances where people that I didn't know knew who I was when I went places. It fed my ego. It was a surreal season of life. But at the same time, I felt an unease that people would not like me if they knew the "real" me. Or the doubt would creep in that I was a fraud both on and off the field.

It reminded me of James 1:23-25, "Anyone who listens to the word but does not do what it says is like a man who looks at his face in a mirror, and after looking at himself, goes away and immediately forgets what he looks like."

I had grown up in the church and had definitely "listened" to the Word. But I certainly was not doing what it said or applying it in my life. The doubt in my mind was very much like the man who forgot what he looked like. And with that I began to sink deeper and deeper into my sin. I lost my virginity as a senior in high school. That, I feel, was the start of the most precipitous fall. From that time forward I just wanted to feel something. I was "chasing the wind." It did not matter what success I had in baseball or what success I was having with women. I was filling a void (or trying to) with things that could not fill it. Only God could do that.

By my senior year in college, my body had essentially called it quits. I spent more time in a trainer's room that year that all my previous years combined. It was a harsh reality that even if I wanted to keep playing, my shoulder especially, would not allow it. It was a time where I truly didn't know who I was. I had lost my identity. My identity was centered in a sport that could be taken away at a moment's notice and in what attention I received from other people. And when that identity was removed, my world came crashing down and I felt like I was in a tailspin. I was partying, sleeping around, got pulled over for suspicion of a DUI and spent the night in jail.

It was at this moment that I hit a bottom and finally felt the prick of the Holy Spirit over me for the first time in many years. I had to start making some serious changes and put in the hard work of getting myself right, or I might end up dead in a ditch somewhere. I separated myself from many of the toxic friendships that I had. I started going to church again and it was just a few months later that I was invited to stand up in a wedding for an old friend that would change the trajectory of my life forever.

Cassidy has touched on many of the specifics of us meeting and the whirlwind romance that we experienced both that first weekend and the year that followed but what she did not share was the fact that as of us meeting I was empowered to continue down a path of positive changes. I no longer felt like I needed to live the old life. I felt a peace that I had found the person that would "complete me." I used to tell myself when I was living in sin that, "This is what I am doing now, but it's not who I will be later on in life." I treated it as though it was a faucet that I could turn on and off. And of course, once we met and started dating, I turned it off and lived on as though nothing had ever happened. I was fooling myself and everyone else around me. The mask was on in full force. Even when asked, I could not come to admit the sins of my past. The problem was that I traded an identity in partying, porn and chasing women, for finding my identity in a single person. Still wrong, it was just a different focus. I should have placed my identity in Christ. Despite all my wrong intentions, I had a year of sobriety based on the highs of a new love and the excitement that came with it.

When Cassidy started unpacking her memories of sexual abuse within the first few months of our marriage, and family confrontations arose, our arguments got more and more explosive. As a person who historically had not done well with conflict, I returned to an "old friend" for comfort. The enemy was waiting for me, with my sin, with open arms. It was not Cassidy's fault that I fell back into sin, I take the full responsibility for that. Part of my problem was that I too, placed my hope and trust in a person. Cassidy and I both were looking at each other to heal us, instead of looking to Christ. When I was let down, I turned to something that would bring me a quick satisfaction to numb the pain, albeit temporary comfort. That's where a relationship with the Lord is so important. That is why Solomon was "chasing the wind." It didn't matter what I had accomplished in baseball. It did not matter what I had accomplished in business. It didn't matter how many friends I had or who found me desirable. EVERYTHING else outside of Christ is temporary. I cannot be made full, and I cannot be made whole by anything of this world.

> *"Since then, you have been raised with Christ, set your hearts on things above, where Christ is, seated at the right hand of God."*
>
> **COLOSSIANS 3:1 NIV**

That is definitely NOT what I was focused on. People will always let you down. It's just a matter of time. What I could not do through all of this was be honest with Cassidy that I was struggling. I couldn't shake the mask that I had made for myself. I was so very worried about appearance that I could not admit the sin even when it was presented in front of me. Pathetic? Yes, but so telling of where many of our young men are today. We have come through life more concerned of what people think of us than who is the real man behind closed doors. What I have learned through this is that when I am weak then He is strong. My help comes from the Lord. I cannot do this alone. I NEED HIM!

"Do not lie to each other, since you have taken off your old self with is practices and have put on the new self, which is being renewed in knowledge in the image of its Creator."

COLOSSIANS 3:1 ESV

After many half-hearted and failed attempts to obtain sobriety, I was faced with a choice. I could continue in my ways which would certainly lead to death, or I could start to make the painful steps that might bring about real and lasting change.

I started to see a counselor which then led me to a men's sobriety group. I had hit bottom. What an embarrassment I thought I was. The shame was like a cloak. I had lost my wife and my children who left for several weeks to Florida. As I started to attend the meetings, I found it helpful to talk to other men who also struggled with sexual sin and temptation. I was finally able to start peeling back the onion!

One of the most important things I have learned in this journey is that what we cannot talk about has power over us. If there is something in my life that I feel awkward or uncomfortable talking about, that is a sign that there is still some work that I need to do in that area. We NEED accountability in our lives. I don't care if you are on your first day as a believer, or the pastor of a mega-church. Men without accountability are playing a game of roulette that will eventually ruin their lives. It is just a matter of time. I don't think people plan to fail, as much as they fail to plan.

All sin falls under one of three categories:

The lust of the eyes.

The lust of the flesh.

The pride of life.

I had to make major changes in my life to achieve sobriety. First thing we did was get rid of cable. I gave my wife full access to my phone at any time. I put accountability software on my computers, tablets, and phone. If I had nothing to hide, then it would not matter if she saw what I was doing. I could not leave anything to chance. I could not afford to lock up the house, so to speak, and leave the back door open for the devil to sneak in, not even a crack.

I think many times we forget that the "wages of our sin is death" (Romans 6:23).

In this case, I had to start realizing that my sin was

KILLING my marriage. I had to put it to death, in a figurative sense, before it killed me.

As I said before, if I had not gotten my sin under control, I would probably be lying dead in a ditch somewhere. While some might say that is a bit over-dramatic, I would tell you it is that detrimental. Every person sets out on a journey with a destination in mind. Each misstep takes you off your directed path and places you on a new trajectory. Continued redirection sends you down a path completely different than the one you started on. That is what sin does to us. I can see clearly where every adulterer, rapist or murderer came from. It was not one decision that led them down that path. It was a series of poor decisions. Either they did not know how to redirect themselves, or they willfully chose not to.

Christ is our true north. He is our compass that leads us into paths of righteousness. I may stumble and fall, but if I have my eyes on my Savior, I have a chance to re-calibrate. If I am void of the Savior, then I will sink further and further into my sin. I will need harder drugs or more provocative things to temporarily satisfy. It does not matter if it is alcohol, drugs, sex, pornography, or power. The lust of the flesh is never satisfied. That is why Solomon fell. He took his eyes off the Lord. This is why I fell, too.

By the grace of God, January 20, 2013, is a sobriety date that I can (as Phil Wickham's song says) take a step back and say, "Look where I am standing now!" Only by the power of Jesus Christ has our marriage been restored! Only by the power of the redeeming blood of Jesus has our relationship been made whole. On top of that, we have been able to help many other couples who have gone down similar paths. One thing that we want to be is a resource for others. We want to use the pain we've gone through to help in a time of hopelessness.

> *"As iron sharpens iron, so one person*
> *sharpens another."*
>
> **PROVERBS 27:17**

We need each other to stay accountable. If you don't have anyone in your life that you are accountable to, can you ask yourself, why not? We tend to have many people in our lives that do not add any value. I recently heard a pastor speaking on this topic and he said that iron sharpens iron but over time with an unequally yoked relationship the blade becomes less sharp. Iron and wood have an adverse effect on one another. One becomes dull and the other becomes damaged. We must build relationships that will lead us in the paths of living water.

CHAPTER 13

Out Of The Ashes

When you are at your lowest and feel like there's no way up, *make* yourself do something for someone else. You don't have to look far to find a need to meet. So many are hurting, and many are going through something more difficult than you are, even in your darkest moments. Help someone else and get your mind off yourself. Self-focus is a trap from the enemy to handicap you. Focusing on your pain will only hinder you. It will keep you stuck. So, I'll say it again because it is your key to happiness: *do something for someone else.* Each act of kindness helps us crawl out of the valley of depression.

Depression takes on *many* forms. In fact, psychologists say there are ten different types of depression. We can find comfort in knowing we are not alone. God is with us and isn't going anywhere. Also, I have found it very helpful to change my scenery. Go outside and take a walk. Get some fresh air and sunshine. My mom always says Vitamin D can heal just about anything.

"The Lord himself goes before you and will be with you; He will never leave you nor forsake you. Do not be afraid; do not be discouraged" (Deuteronomy 31:8).

God was healing my heart and helping me grow in many ways. I couldn't fathom being stretched further. It wasn't until I let go of trying to control Clif *completely*, and entrusted him to the Lord, that he truly became a new man. His salvation as my brother in Christ was more important to me than his role as my husband. I could not control him, his actions, his decisions, nor his recovery. God had to break those strongholds in Clif to build him back up to be the godly man He created him to be. He was uprooting addictions and vicious unhealthy cycles in each of our lives.

We both were seeing counselors and underwent EMDR therapy, which is modality to help alleviate the stress associated with traumatic events. It helped me immensely. I asked the Lord to uncover all I *needed* to know about my history of sexual abuse, no more or less. He healed my deep wound and helped me forgive those individuals who stole my innocence and scarred my heart. Going through EMDR helped me immensely with PTSD. It helped me bring closure to the partial memories of my horrific past. It helped me invite Jesus into the room *each* time the abuse happened and let Him take the pain so I wouldn't try and carry anymore. It also helped me learn to meditate on a safe place to go in my mind when my trauma would arise. My brain and heart needed healing, and the Lord knew this.

He birthed new spiritual gifts in Clif and was bringing them to fruition. Clif came clean about every sexual sin from his past, even those long before he met me. He wanted to be set free and leave no foothold of the enemy in his life any longer. He rededicated his life to Christ and was baptized again. One of my proudest moments as his wife was when he shared part of his testimony with the church before his baptism. He was transparent and approachable to help any other men struggling. We knew what it was like to feel alone on that journey. We decided to use our pain to help others in their marriages. Soon after, we renewed our vows and kept my same diamond, but chose a new band to symbolize a new beginning in our unity.

Out of the ashes a new love arose that was stronger than any love I had ever known. I thought I loved this man on my wedding day, but this love was something altogether different. Walking through this tragedy in our marriage has brought us into a communion with the Lord and each other that nothing could separate.

Anything can be forgiven and restored. God is faithful. When we focus on the Lord we will bloom in the hardest of storms.

"Love never fails."

1 CORINTHIANS 13:8

People will always disappoint or hurt us, just like we let others down at times. We are all born into a sinful nature and we are in need of a Savior. The Holy Spirit can help grow us in the areas we are weak and perfect our personalities. In the moments we are most discouraged, it's important to remember we are never abandoned or betrayed by the Lord. How do I know this? I've seen it! He is faithful every time.

Each of us are given the same 24 hours in a day. We make time for what is important to us. In the sunshine or in the rain, we must take the time to acknowledge what we are thankful for. Take a moment to sit down with a journal and write out blessings in your life and things you give God praise for. Every one of us has blessings in our life. Turn your inner focus to being thankful. When you have a hard day, go back to this blessings journal and reflect on the good things in your life.

I love the saying, "Praise and be raised, or complain and remain." This choice is ours. We don't have control over much that happens in our lives, but we do have the authority to take control of our thought life. What are you focusing on? We also have the choice to not let our circumstances dictate our happiness.

Even in life's greatest tragedies, we can find something to be grateful for. One such thing is the growth opportunities that arise. Realize that you are walking through this season for a reason. Why not grow as much as possible being refined in the fire in the process? The next time a tragedy occurs in your life I encourage you to ask the Lord, "What do you have for me in this?" You have the choice. *Choose* to bloom. If you don't cast your care, you will despair.

> *"Let all bitterness and wrath and anger and clamor and slander be put away from you, along with all malice."*
>
> **EPHESIANS 4:31**

We can find encouragement and gratitude in many powerful Bible verses for depression. There are well over 100. Scripture is a powerful source of inspiration and healing spiritually, mentally, and emotionally. If you don't know what to pray over your situation, pray the scriptures over your life and circumstances. There are answers for every problem we face in His Word.

I encourage you to sit down and pray this simple prayer before you read His Word:

God, I pray that I hear clearly from you. I pray against distractions and hindrances that can come from the voice of others, the voice of the enemy, and the voice of myself. Have your way in me because your way is better than mine.

Soon after returning home from Florida, I faced another challenge. I had been having chronic migraines, ear and nose bleeds, and depression that was hard to shake. We soon found out the inflammation in my brain was having residual side effects. I had a SPECT brain scan done and was shocked to see the damage my brain had suffered. We were reminded again of the miracle work the Lord had done in my life because according to the scan I should have been dealing with partial paralysis on my left side and deafness in my right ear. There were several areas of my brain that were not receiving oxygen and blood flow, so I underwent hyperbaric treatments to help heal those areas. These chamber treatments would force blood flow and oxygen into those injured areas. At some point my skull had shifted and resulted in one of my screws working its way out of one of the plates. This was pushing up into my skin which was left my skin sore, so I underwent surgery to remove that screw and file down the bent plate. I put my hope and trust in the Lord again. I knew he was faithful and would help me handle this challenge as well. And He did.

CHAPTER 14

Golden Season

What a blessing it is when you walk in a golden season of life. Favor comes in many forms and brings unexpected gifts along the way. We had welcomed another precious daughter, Cora, and I was a glowing mother with her arrival. I dealt with hyperemesis again during this pregnancy and Cailynn, Chloe, and Cadence were so helpful and loving to me during this difficult time. The girls were five years old by now, and I think this time helped mature and prepare them for the arrival of their new baby sister. Cora Donyelle brought me a new joy in being a mom. I found out I was pregnant with her when my Papa Camp went into the hospital sick, he died shortly after and I named her in honor of him (Donald). To say I was nervous is an understatement. I was barely keeping my head above water raising the triplets when I found out I was pregnant again. I questioned if I could handle it but the Lord knew exactly what he was doing. Cora helped me blossom into the mother I longed to be. She helped me find new joy in the daily grind of motherhood.

Once again, we were looking for another home, as our lease was coming to an end. We wanted to find a home for our family, a place to put down roots and raise our children. We felt like we were getting nowhere in our search and had looked at almost 100 homes or properties. There were a couple of places we thought might work, but when we went to put in an offer, the door shut in our face. It was a grueling waiting game. We felt like the Lord was very quiet and growing our faith during this drought season.

During this time, the Lord started to speak to me about pulling the girls out of Christian school and homeschooling them. I was fighting Him on this because I felt I was not a good enough mom or smart enough to teach them. He kept speaking to me and then laid it on Clif's heart. After seeking counsel from one of my mentors, Charlana, I knew I was to not delay in obedience, so I pulled them out halfway through the school year. When I did, it was like a weight was lifted off my shoulders.

I encourage you, always be led by peace in your decisions. If you are in doubt, don't. Listen to those promptings from the Holy Spirit. Seek Him and He will lead you and guide you.

> *"Then you will experience God's peace,*
> *which exceeds anything we can understand.*
> *His peace will guard your hearts and minds as*
> *you live in Christ Jesus."*

PHILIPPIANS 4:7

It was on a typical day that we were heading to look at a home and the Lord placed on both Clif's and my heart before we got to the property that this would be our home. We waited on the Lord and His perfect timing in our lives, we didn't settle. It is so important to be on the same page. Don't push your own agenda in marriage. Be a unified front, that is where the Lord's blessings come. This time, we put in our offer and it was accepted! We finally had our home!

We quickly began renovations and construction to make the older home conducive for our family. Mom and dad came up to help for over a month. Mom would stay with the girls during the day teaching them and taking care of the home and meals, while dad and I worked at the homestead sunup to sundown. Many family members and friends came and labored with us to make this new place our home. It meant so much to us. Jerry, Lil, Aunt Karen and Uncle Fred, Clif's brother Brent, and his new wife Cheryl all came several times to help with various tasks around the home and property. Jerry and I worked on putting together a beautifully unique pallet wall in our kitchen, and it was an opportunity to connect and bond with shoulder-to-shoulder time. Even the kids helped where they could. We put our blood, sweat, and tears into this new homestead. The day we moved in was such a blessing.

Sitting on five beautiful acres with a creek and big red barn, it was a dream come true for me. Even down to the detail of turning the attic into our master suit. We bought this property to be a blessing to many, and it has been. We have had the pleasure of holding two weddings here, an engagement, church services, youth events, birthday parties, and prayer meetings. Our children get to run and play in the safety of our property. We've been able to get numerous animals as well, including horses. I grew up with horses and it has been a joy to watch my children experience the benefits of horsemanship. What a gift from the Lord and a blessed childhood they are living.

We sat back and enjoyed the fruits of our labors and basked in the Lord's goodness, and received an even greater gift, our first son was on the way!

Once again, I dealt with hyperemesis with this pregnancy, but it was less severe. I believe because I was carrying a boy this time. Clayton Matthew arrived handsome like daddy with beautiful blue eyes and dimples that made you swoon. Matthew is Clif's middle name as and means gift from Yahweh. We put much thought and prayer into the names of each of our children and have been praying for them since they were in my womb. They are each such a blessing to us! I call Clayton my yummy, because he is so cute I could eat him up! Oh, to have a son, what a cherished gift from the Lord. It is a different love and bond for sure.

To watch my four daughters care for their baby brother is one of the most precious blessings in my life. I am so proud of each of my children and their beautiful hearts and desire to know and serve the Lord. My prayer for them is that their hearts always be open to the Lord no matter what trials and tribulations come their way. As a mom, I do not want them to suffer, but I also know the growth and blessing that comes from relying on our Savior and not our own strengths. Life is not perfect, and we live in a fallen broken world. We try to take negative moments that arise and turn them into teaching opportunities. We are open and honest with them about the importance of our choices. We choose to participate in sin, but we have no control over the consequences that come after.

My children have had to walk through the pain and confusion that comes from broken relationships. Sadly, that is part of life. We are trying to instill in their hearts the importance of loving and forgiving others. We also try to teach them to focus and be grateful for the good and healthy relationships that we do have. It's important to have healthy boundaries and to invest your time, energy, and love wisely. I have often appreciated the optimistic outlook my sister-in-law Cheryl has in life. She encourages others to focus on the positive, shifting their mindset to see where there is progress even if it's not perfect.

It's wise to open up your heart to those who not only love and support you at your best, but also your worst. Find friends who go to war with you in prayer fighting those spiritual battles.

I want to encourage you to find your own circle. We need community, it is crucial to our walk with Christ and fulfilling our calling. We need accountability. Let other people support you and be there to support others as well. When you go through a major failure or trials in life, resist the urge to isolate. There is power in numbers. Every member is vital in the Body of Christ, just like every part of our human body is important.

Have you heard the story of Lazarus in the Bible? I encourage you to take time to read the entire story in John chapter 11. To give you the brief version, Lazarus was very sick, and his sisters sent word to Jesus. He stayed where He was teaching for two more days, then decided to go to him. He waited. In fact, by the time Jesus arrived, Lazarus had been lying in the tomb for four days. Jesus was not fazed by this of course, and went to where they laid him, and proceeded to raise him from the grave. I believe He delayed in this healing to make it an even greater miracle. His timing may not make sense to us, but He sees the whole picture and knows how God will get the greatest glory. Jesus called to Lazarus to come out of the grave, and the dead man came out. Jesus did not run to him, but instead instructed those around him to go and take the grave clothes off. Why? I think he was showing the importance of community. Lazarus needed their help coming out of the grave, literally. And he helped those around him solidify their faith. Bottom line, we need each other.

CHAPTER 15

The Mystery Diagnosis

During my pregnancy with Clayton, I developed strange rashes on the back of my neck, under my arms, and across my chest. After delivery, I had a horrendous reaction all over my stomach and legs. Hives, open sores, and raw skin rashes with no explanation. I ended up seeing four different dermatologists, and having extensive blood work done, with no answers except it was extreme eczema or an allergic reaction. My menstrual cycles became irregular, and my hair started falling out. Fog brain hit me hard. I was tired all the time but couldn't sleep. I would toss and turn all night and deal with hot flashes. It almost felt like I was going into perimenopause, but my OBGYN said I was too young and that wasn't what I was dealing with.

More doctors' appointments, more tests, still no answers. Clif said my skin looked like leprosy! I had open sores going up into my scalp at one time. We got a water purifier, got rid of perfumed items and harmful ingre-dients in our home. I cut out any foods that I showed the slightest allergy to. I started seeing a holistic pro-fessional who thought I was dealing with something autoimmune, and discovered I was producing no pro-gesterone. In fact, all my hormones were out of whack.

So many health issues with no answers. The pain was frustrating and horrible to deal with. My hands bled daily. I was dealing with fatigue. I had restless leg syndrome to go along with the insomnia. My anx-iety felt like something was crawling on my skin. It was like I was trapped under the water, mere inches from the surface, and out of air! That is the best way I can describe anxiety to someone who doesn't struggle with it. I was weary.

> *"This is my comfort in affliction,*
> *that your promise gives me life."*
>
> **PSALM 119:50**

Isn't it ironic that I had been miraculously healed be-fore, and that seemed far from my mind as I was going through more health challenges? This is why it is im-portant to write down answered prayers and meditate on the good things in our lives. When the hard times come, we can go back and focus on things we can give praise over as we remind ourselves of the goodness of our God. When the pain and hurt are overwhelming, learn to be faithful to focus on the blessings around you. The Holy Spirit will guide you in peace and comfort right now in your pain.

My good friend Angela had walked with me through this frustrating season for more than three years and prayed faithfully. She even spent time researching for me. One day she told me she found another woman online with a very similar story and health issues as me. I reached out to this woman and was flooded with hope. It was not until after her third pregnancy that her health issues arose like mine. A light bulb went off.

Back in 2005, I was going through a lot of personal challenges after my accident and surgery. My self-esteem was pretty low and I didn't feel confident in my appearance. Because I developed eating disorders in my younger teen years, it hindered my development as a woman. The sexual abuse I had incurred compounded this issue. I had a negative body image, and I wonder if I have struggled with a small degree of Body Dysmorphic Disorder. With this, I decided to get breast implants for a confidence boost before my wedding. The woman I connected with online also had breast implants and zero issues for more than ten years. I finally had a possible answer to what was going on. *Was my body rejecting the implants?*

Turns out that is exactly what was happening. Ever heard of Breast Implant Illness (BII)? Maybe you have, maybe not. At the time I had not. I think it's important to insert here that I see nothing wrong with plastic surgery. I do think we must be careful why we are doing it, and not to get addicted to trying to perfect our image with numerous procedures. It is essential to learn to be happy with ourselves and appreciate our bodies as they are. I am living proof that having plastic surgery to "fix" something you are insecure about, does NOT lead to happiness. True happiness comes from knowing our value and worth in Christ. There is nothing we can do to make God love us more or love us less. Let that truth sink into your heart. He loves you and accepts you the same at your worst, and at your best.

Once I realized what was going on within my body, I met with an incredible surgeon who specialized in not only removing the implants, but also the scar tissue and cavitation around the implants. Dr. Patel was an answer to prayer. He was so supportive, encouraging, and helpful as we prepared for my explant surgery. In an uncomfortable situation, he helped me feel important and secure going through with the procedures.

We found out that I had diastasis recti (abdominal separation), I believe from carrying the triplets. I also had two abdominal hernias. It was recommended I have surgery to fix this issue at the same time. I had dealt with chronic back and neck pain, and there was hope of this improving by putting my abdominal wall back together.

I was dealing with fear and guilt. I knew it would cost a lot to fix these issues, I felt worried about the expense and time it would take me to recover and not be there for my kids. My good friend, Val, was a big supporter and cheerleader. She not only encouraged me to get the surgery, but she also helped watch all five of my kids during recovery. My high school friend Lauren helped me to see my worth and that having this procedure done was beneficial to my quality of life. I also had help from my cousin Pennie who came up from Florida during my recovery. Also, friends from church showed up in mighty ways to help with my healing journey. I felt showered with love.

I went into major detox after getting those toxic implants out. They had not ruptured, thank the Lord, but did have some black mold in the capsule openings. The rashes roared their ugly head, and Dr. Patel and the sweetest nurse Amy encouraged and helped me through the recovery phase. Within two months my skin completely cleared up! My hormones went back into normal range as well. Breast Implant Illness *is real.* Not only have I gone through it, I have survived it.

I feel most thankful for God's grace through this season. I learned a lot about myself, and even more about Him. The Hebrew word for gracious is *channun.* It's a verb and means to be considerate and show favor.

Even when we mess up or don't make the wisest decisions in our lives, He is faithful with unmerited favor. He freely gives us grace and mercy. Every action of God towards us involves grace. We grow strong in His grace (2 Timothy 2:1). His grace is sufficient for every need we have. It is one of God's greatest gifts to us, but we must accept it.

"Yet God, in His grace, freely makes us right in his sight. He did this through Christ Jesus when he freed us from the penalty of our sins."

ROMANS 3:24 NLV

God's grace is abundant. He continually gives us mercy, love, healing, and forgiveness.

I am so thankful for the redemption of my health

during this trial. Clif has been a huge support of my health journey. What a blessing to have a husband willing to do whatever it takes to help me live a healthy life to the fullest. I am so honored to be married to my best friend. Our love has stood the test of time and becomes stronger with every year.

Jeanne, Tracy, and my parents helped remind me to give myself grace through my recovery. When I was at my lowest points due to the intense detox, they helped me remain patient and let things work their way out in my healing journey. This is crucial. Give yourself time to heal and give yourself grace in the process.

If you have implants and have been dealing with health issues which you cannot figure out the root cause, look into BII. Find a holistic doctor that will help you detox and find a cure, not just ease your symptoms. There is hope! I pray even now that you feel relief and new courage to look into this possible cause for your health challenges.

Bottom line, you are worth it. Your health is an investment, and one to be taken seriously. Our bodies are a temple of the Holy Spirit. We need to be willing to take the necessary steps within our power to live healthy. Sometimes things get harder and more complicated before the breakthrough. Buckle down, hold on and take that first step of faith to get better.

Now, I want to share one more thing about self-esteem. Did you know that there are four different aspects of body image?

1. **Perceptual body image**–the way one sees their body.

2. **Affective body image**–the way one feels about their body.

3. **Cognitive body image**–the way one thinks about their body

4. **Behavioral body image**-the behaviors one engages in as a result of your body image.

It is a challenging, and sometimes a lifelong journey, to have positive body image and acceptance. This is when you accept, appreciate, and respect your body. With the Lord, this is possible. God has given us our bodies for a purpose. It is important we redefine beauty and that starts by renewing our minds.

"Do not conform to the pattern of this world but be transformed by the renewing of your mind. Then you will be able to test and approve what God's will is-his good, pleasing and perfect will" (Romans 12:2 NIV).

When you have a positive body image it leads to a

higher self-esteem, self-acceptance, and a healthier outlook on life. Scripture says that we love others as we love ourselves. Receive God's love for you—that means your body—and be an example of His love to others.

CHAPTER 16

Don't Waste Your Present

One of the best parts about moving up North, after being a Floridian, was finally experiencing the four seasons in full effect. Just like the weather patterns, in our lives, no matter what season you find yourself in, one thing is for sure, the seasons are going to keep changing. In our lives, there are blessings and burdens that come with each season. Your focus is of utmost importance. If you focus on the burdens, you will miss the blessings.

The Bible also talks about the seasons of life and reminds us there is a reason for each season. Ecclesiastes 3 says:

There is a time for everything,
and a season for every activity under the heavens:
a time to be born and a time to die,
a time to plant and a time to uproot,

a time to kill and a time to heal,
a time to tear down and a time to build,
a time to weep and a time to laugh,
a time to mourn and a time to dance,
a time to scatter stones and a time to gather them,
a time to embrace and a time to
refrain from embracing,
a time to search and a time to give up,
a time to keep and a time to throw away,
a time to tear and a time to mend,
a time to be silent and a time to speak,
a time to love and a time to hate,
a time for war and a time for peace.

I remember planting beautiful flowers with my MiMi and Papa Camp in the Springtime. I watched with amazement how they pruned them back and then the new buds would emerge. I can still smell the honeysuckle and orange blossom wafting in the wind, while the honeybees were hard at work. I can still hear my Papa sing one of his favorite hymns and see him clearly in my mind's eye leaning over to kiss MiMi while pulling her in for a dance.

I think back to a fond memory in the heat of sweet summertime. Oh, how I loved to lay in the field watching the puffy clouds go by. I reminisce about picking phlox for my mom to put in a mason jar, and juicy wild blackberries that stained my hands. I hear laughter as my sister and I let our imaginations run wild playing with our plastic horses for hours on end. I smile to picture myself, six years old riding my pony Flicka, wearing my bathing suit, in a full out run across the field, with the wind in my hair and not a care in the world. I smell the leather from packing saddle bags with my sister to ride all day till we heard the dinner bell ring.

And then there is Fall. Fall is my absolute favorite time of year! Fall is the perfect example that change is beautiful. I grew up reading Anne of Green Gables and quote her often, "I'm so glad I live in a world where there are Octobers."

I can almost smell the fresh pine air of visiting with my Granny and Grandpa Ballard on the deck of their mountain house. I can still feel that cool mist blowing off the waterfalls as my brother and I climbed down the rocks to our favorite fishing hole. I can hear Grandpa's contagious laughter fill the air, as we slip and fall in the ice-cold creek. I can feel the warm cup of tea while sitting quietly for a few gold nuggets of wisdom from my Granny while watching those pretty leaves fall.

And then there is winter. I reflect on my past birthdays with bright green Christmas tree cakes made with extra love from my mom. I see the icicles through the window glistening in the sun, that formed in the night because my dad purposely ran the sprinkler to give us Floridians a taste of true winter. I appreciate that this season is a time of forced slow down and much needed rest.

It has been such a fun experience to have snow during the holiday seasons now that I live up North. I never knew you could actually smell snow! There is nothing more perfect to get you in the Christmas spirit than dancing in the snow. I often giggle as I watch my kiddos running around to catch snowflakes on their tongues. One thing I love most about winter is the beautiful snowflakes.

Have you ever looked at a snowflake under a microscope? Or seen pictures of one up close? No two snowflakes are the same. They are the most beautiful work of art! There are many lessons to be learned from these unique little beauties. Each snowflake is imperfectly perfect. As they fall to the ground, they may be blown all around and collide with other snowflakes or objects that alter their shape. Going through their journey they each take their own path. On these paths, the wind blows them to and fro and they adapt and change to reach their destination. Even though the journey changes the snowflake's original shape and size, when it finally lands, it is still uniquely beautiful and shines in the lights. Imperfectly perfect, just like you!

In these imperfections, I implore you to live your life. Be present. Don't wait for the next great moment because those moments are happening right now and will quickly pass you by.

Go after your dreams no matter how crazy or far-fetched they seem. You are capable, and you are worth it. Don't let your fears keep you from reaching your full potential and experiencing all life has to offer you.

God knew you before you were formed in your mother's womb. He chose to have you here, right now, exactly where you are, in this crazy-beautiful journey of life. You have a purpose; you are here for a reason. More than anything, you are here to bloom.

I am a simple girl who has decided to be a willing vessel. I love how the Lord often chooses the weak to show how incredible His power is. I want to leave you with these few reminders to hold close to your heart:

Every day you have been given is a gift.

Every tragedy is a growth opportunity.

Every offense is forgivable.

Every heartache can heal.

Every weakness you struggle with
can become your greatest strength.

Every person in your life is there for a reason,
so give love freely and be a light.

You don't know when your journey will come to an end, so live with no regrets. You are not promised tomorrow, so live with purpose and in freedom. Use your failures to strengthen and build up others. The past is in the past, it's time to move on stronger.

And remember, you do not need the approval of others. God already approves of you.

"And let us run with perseverance the race marked out for us."

HEBREWS 12:1B NIV

It's your life! That's the greatest gift that's been given to you. What will you do with it? What are you waiting for? It's time to bloom where you are planted. Your time is now. *You can! You have! You Will!*

Scriptures for Further Reflection

Scriptures On Dealing With Fear And Anxiety:

"Be strong, do not fear; your God will come, He will come with vengeance; with divine retribution He will come to save you."

ISAIAH 35:4

"Peace I leave with you; My peace I give you. I do not give to you as the world gives. Do not let your hearts be troubled and do not be afraid."

JOHN 14:27

"Therefore do not worry about tomorrow, for tomorrow will worry about itself, each day has enough trouble of its own."

MATTHEW 6:34

"But now, this is what the LORD says – He who created you, Jacob, He who formed you, Israel: 'Do not fear, for I have redeemed you; I have summoned you by name; you are mine.'"

ISAIAH 43:1

"Even though I walk through the darkest valley,
I will fear no evil, for you are with me; your rod
and your staff, they comfort me."

PSALM 23:4

"I sought the Lord, and He answered me and
delivered me from all my fears."

PSALM 34:4

"When anxiety was great within me, Your
consolation brought me joy."

PSALM 94:19

"For I am convinced that neither death nor life,
neither angels nor demons, neither the present
nor the future, nor any powers, neither height nor
depth, nor anything else in all creation, will be
able to separate us from the love of God."

ROMANS 8:38-39

"The LORD is my light and my salvation—whom
shall I fear? The LORD is the stronghold of my
life—of whom shall I be afraid?"

PSALM 27:1

"Be strong and courageous. Do not be afraid
or terrified because of them, for the LORD your
}God goes with you; He will never leave you nor
forsake you."

DEUTERONOMY 31:6

"When I am afraid, I put my trust in You. In God,
whose word I praise—in God I trust and am not
afraid. What can mere mortals do to me?"

PSALM 36:4

"For I am the LORD your God who takes hold of
your right hand and says to you, 'Do not fear;
I will help you.'"

ISAIAH 41:13

"Do not be afraid; you will not be put to shame.
Do not fear disgrace; you will not be humiliated. You
will forget the shame of your youth and remember
no more the reproach of your widowhood."

ISAIAH 54:4

"We demolish arguments and every pretension
that sets itself up against the knowledge of
God, and we take captive every thought to make it

obedient to Christ."

2 CORINTHIANS 10:5

"There is no fear in love. But perfect love drives out fear, because fear has to do with punishment. The one who fears is not made perfect in love."

1 JOHN 4:18

"For the Spirit God gave us does not make us timid, but gives us power, love and self-discipline."

2 TIMOTHY 1:7

"So do not fear, for I am with you; do not be dismayed, for I am your God. I will strengthen you and help you; I will uphold you with my righteous right hand."

ISAIAH 41:10

"Have I not commanded you? Be strong and courageous. Do not be afraid; do not be discouraged, for the LORD your God will be with you wherever you go."

JOSHUA 1:9

"The Spirit you received does not make you slaves,
so that you live in fear again; rather, the Spirit you
received brought about your adoption to sonship.
And by Him we cry, 'Abba, Father.'"

ROMANS 8:15

"Be on your guard; stand firm in the faith;
be courageous; be strong."

1 CORINTHIANS 16:13

"Keep your lives free from the love of money and
be content with what you have, because God has
said, 'Never will I leave you; never will I forsake
you.' So we may say with confidence, 'The Lord is
my helper; I will not be afraid. What can mere
mortals do to me?"

1 PETER 3:13-14

"Who is going to harm you if you are eager to do
good? But even if you should suffer for what is
right,you are blessed. Do not fear their threats;
do not be frightened."

HEBREWS 13:5-6

Scriptures On How To Handle A Crisis:

"This is my comfort in my affliction, that Your promise gives me life."

PSALM 119:50

"The righteous cry out, and the LORD hears them; He delivers them from all their troubles. The LORD is close to the brokenhearted and saves those who are crushed in spirit. A righteous man may have many troubles, but the LORD delivers Him from them all; He protects all his bones, not one of them will be broken."

PSALM 34:17-20

"Finally, brothers and sisters, whatever is true, whatever is noble, whatever is right, whatever is pure, whatever is lovely, whatever is admirable— if anything is excellent or praiseworthy— think about such things."

PHILIPPIANS 5:8

"For the spirit God gave us does not make us timid,
but gives us power, and self-discipline."

2 TIMOTHY 1:7

"For the Lord your God is He who goes with you
to fight for you against your enemies,
to give you victory."

DEUTERONOMY 20:4

"Let us not become weary in doing good,
for at the proper time we will reap a harvest
if we do not give up."

GALATIANS 6:9

"But He said to me, 'My grace is sufficient for you,
for My power is made perfect in weakness.'

Therefore I will boast all the more gladly about
my weaknesses, so that Christ's power may
rest on me."

2 CORINTHIANS 12:9

"But he who stands firm to the end will be saved."

MATTHEW 24:13

"And my God will meet all your needs according to His glorious riches in Christ Jesus."

PHILIPPIANS 4:9

"Be always on the watch, and pray that you may be able to escape all that is about to happen, and that you may be able to stand before the Son of Man."

LUKE 21:36

"What causes fights and quarrels among you? Don't they come from your desires that battle within you? You want something but don't get it. You kill and covet, but you cannot have what you want. You quarrel and fight. You do not have, because you do not ask God."

JAMES 4:1-20

"Do not let your hearts be troubled. Trust in God; trust also in Me. In my Father's house are many rooms; if it were not so, I would have told you. I am going there to prepare a place for you. And if I go and prepare a place for you, I will come back and take you to be with me that you also may be where I am. You know the way to the place where I am going. Thomas said to Him, 'Lord, we don't know where You are going, so how can we know the way?' Jesus answered, 'I am the Way and the Truth and the Life. No one comes to the Father except through Me. If you really knew Me, you would know My Father as well. From now on, you do know Him and have seen Him.' Philip said, 'Lord, show us the Father and that will be enough for us.' Jesus answered, 'Don't you know Me, Philip, even after I have been among you such a long time? Anyone who has seen Me has seen the Father. How can you say, 'Show us the Father?' Don't you believe that I am in the Father, and that the Father is in Me? The words I say to you are not just My own. Rather, it is the Father, living in Me, who is doing His work. Believe Me when I say that I am in the Father and the Father is in Me; or at least believe on the evidence of the miracles themselves. I tell you the truth, anyone who has faith in Me will do what I have been doing. He will do even greater things than these, because I am going to the Father. And I will do whatever you ask in My Name, so that the Son may bring glory to the Father. You may ask Me for anything in My Name, and I will do it. If you love Me, you will obey what I command. And I will ask the Father, and He will give you another Counselor to be with you forever—the Spirit of Truth. The world cannot accept Him, because it neither sees Him nor knows Him. But you know

Him, for He lives with you and will be in you. I will not leave you as orphans; I will come to you. Before long, the world will not see Me anymore, but you will see Me. Because I live, you also will live. On that day you will realize that I am in my Father, and you are in Me, and I am in you. Whoever has My commands and obeys them, He is the one who loves Me. He who loves Me will be loved by my Father, and I too will love him and show Myself to him. Then Judas (not Judas Iscariot) said, 'But, Lord, why do you intend to show yourself to us and not to the world?' Jesus replied, 'If anyone loves Me, he will obey My teaching. My Father will love him, and we will come to him and make our home with him. He who does not love Me will not obey My teaching. These words you hear are not My own; they belong to the Father who sent Me. All this I have spoken while still with you. But the Counselor, the Holy Spirit, whom the Father will send in My Name, will teach you all things and will remind you of everything I have said to you. Peace I leave with you; My peace I give you. I do not give to you as the world gives. Do not let your hearts be troubled and do not be afraid. You heard me say, 'I am going away and I am coming back to you.' If you loved Me, you would be glad that I am going to the Father, for the Father is greater than I. I have told you now before it happens, so that when it does happen you will believe. I will not speak with you much longer, for the prince of this world is coming. He has no hold on Me, but the world must learn that I love the Father and that I do exactly what My Father has commanded Me."

JOHN 14:1-31

"I will extol the LORD at all times; His praise will always be on my lips. My soul will boast in the LORD; let the afflicted hear and rejoice. Glorify the LORD with me; let us exalt His name together. I sought the LORD, and He answered me; He delivered me from all my fears. Those who look to Him are radiant; their faces are never covered with shame. This poor man called, and the LORD heard Him; He saved him out of all his troubles. The angel of the LORD encamps around those who fear Him, and he delivers them. Taste and see that the LORD is good; blessed is the man who takes refuge in Him. Fear the LORD, you His saints, for those who fear him lack nothing. The lions may grow weak and hungry, but those who seek the LORD lack no good thing. Come, My children, listen to Me; I will teach you the fear of the LORD. Whoever of you loves life and desires to see many good days, keep your tongue from evil and your lips from speaking lies. Turn from evil and do good; seek peace and pursue it. The eyes of the LORD are on the righteous and His ears are attentive to their cry; the face of the LORD is against those who do evil, to cut off the memory of them from the earth. The righteous cry out, and the LORD hears them; He delivers them from all their troubles. The LORD is close to the brokenhearted and saves those who are crushed in spirit. A righteous man may have many troubles, but the LORD delivers him from them all; He protects all his bones, not one of them will be broken. Evil will slay the wicked; the foes of the righteous will be condemned. The LORD redeems His servants; no one will be condemned who takes refuge in Him."

PSALM 34:1-22

"I consider that our present sufferings are not worth comparing with the glory that will be revealed in us."

ROMANS 8:18

"Now faith is being sure of what we hope for and certain of what we do not see. This is what the ancients were commended for. By faith we understand that the universe was formed at God's command, so that what is seen was not made out of what was visible. By faith Abel offered God a better sacrifice than Cain did. By faith he was commended as a righteous man, when God spoke well of his offerings. And by faith he still speaks, even though he is dead. By faith Enoch was taken from this life, so that he did not experience death; he could not be found, because God had taken him away. For before he was taken, he was commended as one who pleased God. And without faith it is impossible to please God, because anyone who comes to him must believe that he exists and that he rewards those who earnestly seek him. By faith Noah, when warned about things not yet seen, in holy fear built an ark to save his family. By his faith he condemned the world and became heir of the righteousness that comes by faith. By faith Abraham, when called to go to a place he would later receive as his inheritance, obeyed and went, even though he did not know where he was going. By faith he made his home in the promised land like a stranger in a foreign country; he lived in tents, as did Isaac and Jacob, who were heirs with him of the same promise. For he was looking forward to the city with foundations, whose architect and builder is God. By faith Abraham, even though he was past age—and Sarah herself was barren—was enabled to become a father because he considered him faithful who had made the promise. And so from this one man, and he as good as dead, came descendants as numerous as the stars in the sky and as countless as the sand on the seashore. All these people were still living by faith when they died. They did not receive the things promised; they only saw them and welcomed them from a distance. And they admitted that they were aliens and strangers on earth. People who say such things show that they are looking for a country of their own. If they had been thinking of the country they had left, they would have had opportunity to return. Instead, they were longing for a better country—a heavenly one. Therefore, God is not ashamed to be called their God, for He has prepared a city for them. By faith Abraham, when God tested him, offered Isaac as a sacrifice. He who had received the promises was about to sacrifice his one and only son, even though God had said to him, 'It is through Isaac that your offspring will be reckoned.' Abraham reasoned that God could raise the dead, and figuratively speaking, he did receive Isaac back from death. By faith Isaac blessed Jacob and Esau in regard to their future. By faith Jacob, when he was dying, blessed each of Joseph's sons, and worshiped as he leaned on the top of his staff. By faith Joseph, when his end was near, spoke about the exodus of the Israelites from Egypt and gave instructions about his bones. By faith Moses' parents hid him for three months after he was born, because they saw he was no ordinary child, and they were not afraid of the king's edict. By faith Moses, when he had grown up, refused to be known as the son of Pharaoh's daughter. He chose to be mistreated along with the people of God rather than to enjoy the pleasures of sin for a short time. He regarded disgrace for the sake of Christ as of greater value than the treasures of Egypt, because he was looking ahead to his reward. By faith he left Egypt, not fearing the king's anger; he persevered because he saw him who is invisible. By faith he kept the Passover and the sprinkling of blood, so that the destroyer of the firstborn would not touch the firstborn of Israel. By faith the people passed through the Red Sea as on dry land; but when the Egyptians tried to do so, they were drowned. By faith the walls of Jericho fell, after the people had marched around them for seven days. By faith the prostitute Rahab, because she welcomed the spies, was not killed with those who were disobedient. And what more shall I say? I do not have time to tell about Gideon, Barak, Samson, Jephthah, David, Samuel and the prophets, who through faith conquered kingdoms, administered justice, and gained what was promised; who

shut the mouths of lions, quenched the fury of the
flames, and escaped the edge of the sword; whose
weakness was turned to strength; and who became
powerful in battle and routed foreign armies. Women
received back their dead, raised to life again. Others
were tortured and refused to be released, so that they
might gain a better resurrection. Some faced jeers
and flogging, while still others were chained and
put in prison. They were stoned; they were sawed in
two; they were put to death by the sword. They went
about in sheepskins and goatskins, destitute, per-
secuted and mistreated—the world was not worthy
of them. They wandered in deserts and mountains,
and in caves and holes in the ground. These were all
commended for their faith, yet none of them received
what had been promised. God had planned something
better for us so that only together with us would they
be made perfect."

HEBREWS 11:1-40

"The LORD is my Shepherd, I shall not be in want.
He makes me lie down in green pastures, He leads
me beside quiet waters, He restores my soul.
He guides me in paths of righteousness for His
Name's sake. Even though I walk through the valley
of the shadow of death, I will fear no evil, for You

are with me; Your rod and Your staff, they comfort me. You prepare a table before me in the presence of my enemies. You anoint my head with oil; my cup overflows. Surely goodness and mercy will follow me all the days of my life, and I will dwell in the house of the LORD forever."

PSALM 23:1-6

"I have said these things to you, that in Me you may have peace. In the world you will have tribulation. But take heart, I have overcome the world."

JOHN 16:33

"When you find Me, you find life, real life, to say nothing of God's good pleasure. But if you wrong Me, you damage your very soul; when you reject Me, you're flirting with death."

PROVERBS 8:35

"Consider it pure joy, my brothers and sisters, whenever you face trials of many kinds. Because you know that the testing of your faith produces perseverance. Let perseverance finish its

work so that you may be mature and complete,
not lacking anything."

JAMES 1:2-4

Scriptures On Relationships:

"For when two or three gather in my name,
there
I am with them."

MATTHEW 18:20

"As iron sharpens iron, so one person
sharpens another."

PROVERBS 27:17

"And let us consider how we may spur one another
on toward love and good deeds, not giving up
meeting together, as some are in the habit of doing,
but encouraging one another-and all the more as you
see the day approaching."

HEBREWS 10:24-25

"The Lord is on my side; I will not fear. What can
man do to me?"

PSALM 118:6

"Many are the afflictions of the righteous,
but the Lord delivers him out of them all. We must
let the Lord defend us and trust the truth will
come out one day."

PSALM 34:19

"Leave your troubles with the Lord, and He will defend you; He never lets honest people be defeated."

PSALM 55:22

"For if you forgive other people when they sin
against you, your heavenly Father will
also forgive you."

MATTHEW 6:14

"Do not judge, and you will not be judged. Do not
condemn, and you will not be condemned.
Forgive, and you will be forgiven."

LUKE 6:37

"Be ready to do whatever is good, to slander no one, to be peaceable and considerate, and always to be gentle toward everyone. At one time we too were foolish, disobedient, deceived and enslaved by all kinds of passions and pleasures. We lived in malice and envy, being hated and hating one another. But when the kindness and love of God our Savior appeared, He saved us, not because of righteous things we had done, but because of His mercy. He saved us through the washing of rebirth and renewal by the Holy Spirit, whom He poured out on us generously through Jesus Christ our Savior, so that, having been justified by His grace, we might become heirs having the hope of eternal life. This is a trustworthy saying. And I want you to stress these things, so that those who have trusted in God may be careful to devote themselves to doing what is good. These things are excellent and profitable for everyone."

TITUS 3:1B-8

"One who has unreliable friends soon comes to ruin, but there is a friend who sticks closer than a brother."

PROVERBS 18:24

"Suppose someone falls down. Then his friend can help him up. But suppose the man who falls down doesn't have anyone to help him up. Then feel sorry for him."

ECCLESIASTES 4:10 NIRV

"Carry each other's burdens, and in this way you will fulfill the law of Christ."

GALATIANS 6:2

"Greater love has no one than this: to lay down one's life for one's friends."

JOHN 15:13

"Above all, keep loving one another earnestly, since love covers a multitude of sins. Show hospitality to one another without grumbling. As each has received a gift, use it to serve one another, as good stewards of God's varied grace."

1 PETER 4:8-10

"One who forgives an affront fosters friendship, but one who dwells on disputes will alienate a friend."

PROVERBS 17:9

"Love is patient, love is kind. It is not jealous, is not pompous, it is not inflated, it is not rude, it does not seek its own interest, it is not quick-tempered, it does not brood over injury (or keep records of wrong), it does not rejoice over wrongdoing but rejoices with truth. It bears all things, believes all things, hopes all things, and endures all things."

1 CORINTHIANS 13:4-7

"Hatred stirs old quarrels, but love overlooks insults."

PROVERBS 10:12

"Be kind and compassionate to one another, forgiving each other, just as in Christ God forgave you. We are called and commanded to forgive. It is crucial to our walk with God, and for victory in our lives."

EPHESIANS 4:32

"Blessed is the man who remains steadfast under trial, for when he has stood the test of time he will receive the crown of life, which God has promised to those who love Him."

JAMES 1:12

"Listen to advice and accept instruction, and in the end you will be wise. Many are the plans in a man's heart, but it is the Lord's purpose that prevails."

PROVERBS 19:20-21

"The way of a fool seems right to him, but a wise man listens to advice."

PROVERBS 12:15

Scriptures On Your Identity In Christ:

"For who knows if you were born for such a time as this."

ESTHER 4:14

"For I know the plans I have for you declares the Lord. Plans to prosper you and not to harm you, plans to give you hope and a future."

JEREMIAH 29:11

"Therefore, if anyone is in Christ, he is a new creation. The old has passed away; behold, the new has come."

2 THESSALONIANS 5:17

"We were buried therefore with Him by baptism into death, in order that, just as Christ was raised from the dead by the glory of the Father, we too might walk in newness of life."

ROMANS 6:4

"Put off your old self, which belongs to your former manner of life and is corrupt through deceitful desires, and be renewed in the spirit of your minds, and put on the new self, created after the likeness of God in true righteousness and holiness."

EPHESIANS 4:22-24

"And have put on the new self, which is being renewed in knowledge in the image of its Creator."

COLOSSIANS 3:10

"So you are no longer a slave, but God's child; and since you are His child, God has made you also an heir."

GALATIANS 4:7

"I have told you this so that My joy may be in you and that your joy may be complete."

JOHN 15:11

"But because of His great love for us, God, who is rich in mercy, made us alive with Christ even when we were dead in transgressions—it is by grace you have been saved."

EPHESIANS 2:4-5

"Now if we are children, then we are heirs—heirs of God and co-heirs with Christ, if indeed we share in His sufferings in order that we may also share in his glory."

ROMANS 8:17

"But you are a chosen people, a royal priesthood, a holy nation, God's special possession, that you may declare the praises of Him who called you out of darkness into His wonderful light. Once you were not a people, but now you are the people of God; once you had not received mercy, but now you have received mercy."

1 PETER 2:9-10

""Now if you will indeed obey My voice and keep My covenant, you will be My treasured possession out of all the nations—for the whole earth is Mine."

EXODUS 19:5

"Do you not know that your bodies are temples of the Holy Spirit, who is in you whom you have received from God? You are not your own; you were bought at a price. Therefore, honor God with your bodies."

1 CORINTHIANS 6:19-20

"So do not fear, for I am with you; do not be dismayed for I am your God. I will strengthen you and help you; I will uphold you with my righteous right hand."

ISAIAH 41:10

"And we know that in all things God works for the good of those who love Him, who have been called according to his purpose. For those God foreknew He also predestined to be conformed to the image of His Son, that He might be the first-born among many brothers and sisters. And those

He predestined, He also called; those He called, He also justified; those He justified, He also glorified. What then shall we say in response to these things? If God is for us, who can be against us? In all these things we are more than conquerors through Him who loved us. For I am convinced that neither death nor life, neither angels nor demons, neither present nor the future, nor any powers, neither height nor depth, nor anything else in creation, will be able to separate us from the love of God that is in Christ Jesus our Lord."

ROMANS 8:28-31;37-39

"But those who hope in the Lord will renew their strength. They will soar on wings like eagles; they will run and not grow weary; they will walk and not be faint."

ISAIAH 40:31

"Therefore, do not throw away your confidence, which has a great reward. For you have need of endurance, so that when you have done the will of God, you may receive what was promised."

HEBREWS 10:35-36

"But blessed is the one whose trust is in the Lord,
whose confidence is in him."

JEREMIAH 17:7

"The Lord is a shelter for the oppressed,
a refuge in times of trouble."

PSALM 9:9

"Because of His grace He made us right in
His sight and gave us confidence that we will
inherit eternal life."

TITUS 3:7

"Therefore take up the whole armor of God, that
you may be able to withstand in the evil day, and
having done all, to stand firm."

EPHESIANS 6:13

"Let us then approach God's throne of grace with
confidence, so that we may receive mercy and find
grace to help us in our time of need."

HEBREWS 4:16

"Do not conform to the pattern of this world, but be transformed by the renewing of your mind. Then you will be able to test and approve what God's will is His good, pleasing and perfect will."

ROMANS 12:2

"For the spirit God gave us does not make us timid, but gives us power, love, and self-discipline."

2 TIMOTHY 1:7

"For the Lord your God is he who goes with you to fight for you against your enemies, to give you victory."

DEUTERONOMY 20:4

"Do not be conformed to this world, but be transformed by the renewal of your mind, that by testing you may discern what is the will of God."

ROMANS 12:2

"You, Lord, are forgiving and good, abounding in love to all who call to You."

PSALM 86:5

"The mind governed by the flesh is death, but the

mind governed by the Spirit is life and peace."

ROMANS 8:6

"Your beauty should not come from outward adornment, such as elaborate hairstyles and the wearing of gold jewelry or fine clothes. Rather, it should be that of your inner self, the unfading beauty of a gentle and quiet spirit, which is great worth in God's sight."

1 PETER 3:3-4

"Charm is deceptive, and beauty is fleeting; but a woman who fears the Lord is praised."

PROVERBS 31:30

"The Lord is a stronghold for the oppressed, a stronghold in times of trouble."

PSALM 9:9

"The Lord directs the steps of the godly. He delights in every detail of their lives. Though they may stumble, they will never fall, for the Lord holds them by His hand."

PSALM 37:23-24

"The Lord, the Lord, the compassionate and gracious God, slow to anger, abounding in love and faithfulness."

EXODUS 34:6

"For from His fullness we have all received, grace upon grace."

JOHN 1:16

"I praise You because I am fearfully and wonderfully made; Your works are wonderful, I know that full well."

PSALM 139:14

"Oh taste and see that the Lord is good, blessed is the one who takes refuge in Him."

PSALM 34:8

Scriptures On Healing:

"Heal me, O Lord, and I will be healed; save me and I will be saved, for You are the One I praise."

JEREMIAH 17:14

"Is anyone among you sick? Let them call the elders of the church to pray over them and anoint them with oil in the name of the Lord. And the prayer offered in faith will make the sick person well; the Lord will raise them up. If they have sinned, they will be forgiven."

JAMES 5:14-15

"LORD my God, I called to You for help, and You healed me."

PSALM 30:2

"Come to me, all you who are weary and burdened, and I will give you rest."

MATTHEW 11:28

"'But I will restore you to health and heal your wounds', declares the LORD..."

JEREMIAH 30:17

"My son, give attention to my words; incline your ear to my sayings. Do not let them depart from your eyes; keep them in the midst of your heart; for they

are life to those who find them, and health to all
their flesh."

PROVERBS 4:20-22

"A cheerful heart is good medicine, but a crushed
spirit dries up the bones."

PROVERBS 17:22

"And my God will meet all your needs according to
the riches of His glory in Christ Jesus."

PHILIPPIANS 4:19

"You restored me to health and let me live. Surely it
was for my benefit that I suffered such anguish. In
Your love you kept me from the pit of destruction;
You have put all my sins behind Your back."

ISAIAH 38:16-17

"He gives power to the weak, and to those who have
no might He increases strength...Those who wait
on the LORD shall renew their strength; they shall
mount up with wings like eagles, they shall run and
not be weary, they shall walk and not faint."

ISAIAH 40:29-31

"He Himself bore our sins in his body on the tree,
that we might die to sin and live to righteousness.
By His wounds you have been healed."

1 PETER 2:24

"Beloved, I pray that all may go well with you
and that you may be in good health, as it goes
well with your soul."

3 JOHN 1:2

"LORD, be gracious to us; we long for You.
Be our strength every morning, our salvation
in time of distress."

ISAIAH 33:2

"Therefore confess your sins to each other and pray
for each other so that you may be healed.

The prayer of a righteous person is
powerful and effective."

JAMES 5:16

"Trust in the LORD with all your heart, and lean
not on your own understanding. In all your ways
submit to Him, and He will make your paths

straight. Do not be wise in your own eyes; fear the LORD and shun evil. This will bring health to your body and nourishment to your bones."

PROVERBS 3:5-8

"Not only that, but we rejoice in our sufferings, knowing that suffering produces endurance, and endurance produces character, and character produces hope..."

ROMANS 5:3-4

"Worship the LORD your God, and His blessing will be on your food and water. I will take away sickness from among you..."

EXODUS 23:25

"The righteous cry out, and the LORD hears them; He delivers them from all their troubles. The LORD is close to the brokenhearted and saves those who are crushed in spirit."

PSALM 34:17-18

"But He said to me, 'My grace is sufficient for you, for My power is made perfect in weakness.' Therefore, I will boast all the more gladly

of my weaknesses, so that Christ's power
may rest on me."

2 CORINTHIANS 12:9

"Gracious words are a honeycomb, sweet to the
soul and healing to the bones."

PROVERBS 16:24

"Praise the LORD, my soul, and forget not all His
benefits —who forgives all your sins and heals all
your diseases, who redeems your life from the pit
and crowns you with love and compassion."

PROVERBS 103:2-4

"The Lord sustains them on their sickbed and
restores them from their bed of illness."

PSALM 41:3

Scriptures On Depression:

"The Lord is a refuge for the oppressed, a stronghold in times of trouble."

PSALM 9:9

"For His anger lasts only a moment, but His favor lasts a lifetime; weeping may stay for the night, but rejoicing comes in the morning."

PSALM 30:5

"You turned my wailing into dancing; you removed my sackcloth and clothed me with joy."

PSALM 30:11

"He lifted me out of the slimy pit, out of the mud and mire; He set my feet on a rock and gave me a firm place to stand."

PSALM 40:2

"Answer me quickly, Lord; my spirit fails. Do not hide Your face from me or I will be like those who go down to the pit. Let the morning bring me word of Your unfailing love, for I have put my trust in You. Show me the way I should go, for to You I entrust my life. Rescue me from my enemies, Lord, for I hide myself in You."

PSALM 143:7-9

"Come to Me, all you who are weary and burdened, and I will give you rest. Take My yoke upon you and learn from Me, for I am gentle and humble in heart, and you will find rest for your souls. For My yoke is easy and My burden is light."

MATTHEW 11:28-30

"The thief comes only to steal and kill and destroy; I have come that they may have life, and have it to the full."

JOHN 10:10

"Finally, brothers and sisters, whatever is true, whatever is noble, whatever is right, whatever is pure, whatever is lovely, whatever is admirable–if anything is excellent or praiseworthy–think about such things."

PHILIPPIANS 4:8

"The LORD Himself goes before you and will be with you; He will never leave you nor forsake you. Do not be afraid; do not be discouraged."

DEUTERONOMY 31:8

"The righteous cry out, and the LORD hears them; He delivers them from all their troubles."

PSALM 34:17

"I waited patiently for the LORD; He turned
to me and heard my cry. He lifted me out of the
slimy pit, out of the mud and mire; He set my feet
on a rock and gave me a firm place to stand.
He put a new song in my mouth, a hymn of praise
to our God. Many will see and fear the LORD and put
their trust in Him."

PSALM 40:1-3

"But you, LORD, are a shield around me, my glory,
the One who lifts my head high."

PSALM 3:3

"Why, my soul, are you downcast? Why so
disturbed within me? Put your hope in God,

for I will yet praise Him, my Savior and my God."

PSALM 42:11

"Humble yourselves, therefore, under God's
mighty hand, that He may lift you up in due time.
Cast all your anxiety on Him because
He cares for you."

1 PETER 5:6-7

"Praise be to the God and Father of our Lord Jesus Christ, the Father of compassion and the God of all comfort, who comforts us in all our troubles, so that we can comfort those in any trouble with the comfort we ourselves receive from God."

2 CORINTHIANS 1:3-4

"Dear friends, do not be surprised at the fiery ordeal that has come on you to test you, as though something strange were happening to you. But rejoice in as much as you participate in the sufferings of Christ, so that you may be overjoyed when His glory is revealed."

1 PETER 4:12-13

"The LORD makes firm the steps of the one who delights in Him; though he may stumble, he will not fall, for the LORD upholds him with His hand."

PSALM 37:23-24

Scriptures On Truth:

"Call to Me and I will answer you and tell you great

and unsearchable things you do not know."
JEREMIAH 33:3

"For there is nothing hidden that will not be disclosed, and nothing concealed that will not be known or brought out into the open."
LUKE 8:17

"Whoever conceals their sins does not prosper, but the one who confesses and renounces them finds mercy."
PROVERBS 28:13

"These are the things God has revealed to us by His Spirit. The Spirit searches all things,

even the deep things of God."
1 CORINTHIANS 2:10

"Stand firm then, with the belt of truth buckled around your waist, with the breastplate of righteousness in place."
EPHESIANS 6:14

"Dear children, let us not love with words or speech but with actions and in truth."

1 JOHN 3:18

"These are the things you are to do: Speak the truth to each other and render true and sound judgment in your courts."

ZECHARIAH 8:16

"Love is patient, love is kind. It does not envy, it does not boast, it is not proud. It does not dishonor others, it is not self-seeking, it is not easily angered, it keeps no record of wrongs. Love does not delight in evil but rejoices with the truth."

1 CORINTHIANS 13:4-6

"Sanctify them by the truth; Your Word is truth."

JOHN 17:17

"We are from God, and whoever knows God listens to us; but whoever is not from God does not listen to us. This is how we recognize the Spirit of Truth and the spirit of falsehood."

1 JOHN 4:6

Scriptures On Dealing With Offense:

"Good sense makes one slow to anger, and it is his glory to overlook an offense."

PROVERBS 19:11

"Do not take to heart all the things that people say, lest you hear your servant cursing you. Your heart knows that many times you yourself have cursed others."

ECCLESIASTES 7:21-22

"A brother offended is more unyielding than a strong city, and quarreling is like the bars of a castle."

PROVERBS 18:19

"If your brother sins against you, go and tell him his fault, between you and him alone. If he listens to you, you have gained your brother. But if he does not listen, take one or two others along with you, that every charge may be established by the evidence of two or three witnesses. If he refuses to listen to them, tell it to the church. And if he refuses

to listen even to the church, let him be to you as a
Gentile and a tax collector."

MATTHEW 18:15-17

"Pay attention to yourselves! If your brother sins,
rebuke him, and if he repents, forgive him,
and if he sins against you seven times in the day,
and turns to you seven times, saying, 'I repent,'
you must forgive him."

LUKE 17:3-4

"With all humility and gentleness, with patience,
bearing with one another in love eager to maintain
the unity of the Spirit in the bond of peace."

EPHESIANS 4:2-3

"For where jealousy and selfish ambition exist, there
will be disorder and every vile practice."

JAMES 3:16

"There are six things that the LORD hates, seven
that are an abomination to Him: haughty eyes, a
lying tongue, and hands that shed innocent blood,
a heart that devises wicked plans, feet that make

haste to run to evil, a false witness who breathes out lies, and one who sows discord among brothers."

PROVERBS 6:16-19

"You shall not take vengeance or bear a grudge against the sons of your own people, but you shall love your neighbor as yourself: I am the LORD."

LEVITICUS 19:18

"When He was reviled, He did not revile in return; when He suffered, He did not threaten, but continued entrusting Himself to him who judges justly."

1 PETER 2:23

"If I speak in the tongues of men and of angels, but have not love, I am a noisy gong or a clanging cymbal. And if I have prophetic powers, and understand all mysteries and all knowledge, and if I have all faith, so as to remove mountains, but have not love, I am nothing. If I give away all I have, and if I deliver up my body to be burned, but have not love, I gain nothing. Love is patient and kind; love does not envy or boast; it is not arrogant or rude. It does not insist on its own way; it is not irritable or resentful; it does not rejoice at wrongdoing, but rejoices with the truth. Love bears all things, believes all things, hopes all things, endures all things. Love never ends. As for prophecies, they will pass away; as for tongues, they will cease; as for knowledge, it will pass away. For we know in part and we prophesy in part, but when the perfect comes, the partial will pass away. When I was a child, I spoke like a child, I thought like a child, I reasoned like a child. When I became a man, I gave up childish ways. For now we see in a mirror dimly, but then face to face. Now I know in part; then I shall know fully, even as I have been fully known. So now faith, hope, and love abide, these three; but the greatest of these is love."

1 CORINTHIANS 13:1-13

"Know this, my beloved brothers: let every person be quick to hear, slow to speak, slow to anger."

JAMES 1:19

"Judge not, that you be not judged. For with the judgment you pronounce you will be judged, and with the measure you use it will be measured to you. Why do you see the speck that is in your brother's eye, but do not notice the log that is in your own eye? Or how can you say to your brother, 'Let me take the speck out of your eye,' when there is the log in your own eye? You hypocrite, first take the log out of your own eye, and then you will see clearly to take the speck out of your brother's eye."

MATTHEW 7:1-5

"Brothers, if anyone is caught in any transgression, you who are spiritual should restore him in a spirit of gentleness. Keep watch on yourself, lest you too be tempted. Bear one another's burdens, and so fulfill the law of Christ. For if anyone thinks he is something, when he is nothing, he deceives himself."

GALATIANS 6:1-3

"Better is open rebuke than hidden love. Faithful are the wounds of a friend; profuse are the kisses of an enemy."

PROVERBS 27:5-6

"Therefore be imitators of God, as beloved children. And walk in love, as Christ loved us and gave himself up for us, a fragrant offering and sacrifice to God. But sexual immorality and all impurity or covetousness must not even be named among you, as is proper among saints. Let there be no filthiness nor foolish talk nor crude joking, which are out of place, but instead let there be thanksgiving. For you may be sure of this, that everyone who is sexually immoral or impure, or who is covetous (that is, an idolater), has no inheritance in the kingdom of Christ and God. Let no one deceive you with empty words, for because of these things the wrath of God comes upon the sons of disobedience. Therefore do not become partners with them; for at one time you were darkness, but now you are light in the Lord. Walk as children of light (for the fruit of light is found in all that is good and right and true), and try to discern what is pleasing to the Lord. Take no part in the unfruitful works of darkness, but instead expose them. For it is shameful even to speak of the things that they do in secret. But when anything is exposed by the light, it becomes visible, for anything that becomes visible is light. Therefore it says, 'Awake, O sleeper, and arise from the dead, and Christ will shine on you. Look carefully then how you walk, not as unwise but as wise, making the best use of the time, because the days are evil.' Therefore do not be foolish, but understand what the will of the Lord is. And do not get drunk with wine, for that is debauchery, but be filled with the Spirit, addressing one another in psalms and hymns and spiritual songs, singing and making melody to the Lord with your heart, giving thanks always and for everything to God the Father in the name of our Lord Jesus Christ, submitting to one another out of reverence for Christ. Wives, submit to your own husbands, as to the Lord. For the husband is the head of the wife even as Christ is the head of the church, his body, and is himself its Savior. Now as the church submits to Christ, so also wives should submit in everything to their husbands. Husbands, love your wives, as Christ loved the church and gave himself up for her, that he might sanctify her, having cleansed her by the washing of water with the word, so that he might present the church to himself in splendor, without spot or wrinkle or any such thing, that she might be holy and without blemish. In the same way husbands should love their wives as their own bodies. He who loves his wife loves himself. For no one ever hated his own flesh, but nourishes and cherishes it, just as Christ does the church, because we are members of his body. Therefore a man shall leave his father and mother and hold fast to his wife, and the two shall become one flesh. This mystery is profound, and I am saying that it refers to Christ and the church. However, let each one of you love his wife as himself, and let the wife see that she respects her husband."

EPHESIANS 5:1-33

"Whoever covers an offense seeks love, but he who repeats a matter separates close friends."

PROVERBS 17:9

"And the Lord's servant must not be quarrelsome but kind to everyone, able to teach, patiently enduring evil, correcting his opponents with gentleness. God may perhaps grant them repentance leading to a knowledge of the truth, and they may come to their senses and escape from the snare of the devil, after being captured by him to do his will."

2 TIMOTHY 2:24-26

Scriptures For Strength:

"I can do all things through Christ who strengthens me."

PHILIPPIANS 4:13

"Fear not, for I am with you; be not dismayed, for I am your God; I will strengthen you, I will help you, I will uphold you with my righteous right hand."

ISAIAH 41:1

"But they who wait for the Lord shall renew their strength; they shall mount up with wings like eagles; they shall run and not be weary; they shall walk and not faint."

ISAIAH 40:31

"The Lord is my strength and my song, and He has become my salvation; this is my God, and I will praise Him, my father's God, and I will exalt Him."

EXODUS 15:2

"Finally, be strong in the Lord and in the strength of His might."

EPHESIANS 6:10

"Look to the Lord and His strength; seek His face always.

1 CHRONICLES 16:11

"Have I not commanded you? Be strong and courageous. Do not be afraid; do not be discouraged, for the Lord your God will be with you wherever you go."

JOSHUA 1:9

"For the Spirit God gave us does not make us timid, but gives us power, love and self-discipline."

2 TIMOTHY 1:7

"The Sovereign Lord is my strength; He makes my feet like the feet of a deer, He enables me to tread on the heights."

HABAKKUK 3:19

"If anyone speaks, they should do so as one who speaks the very words of God. If anyone serves, they should do so with the strength God provides, so that in all things God may be praised through Jesus Christ. To Him be the glory and the power for ever and ever."

1 PETER 4:11

"The Lord is my strength and my defense; He has become my salvation."

PSALM 118:4

"The Lord is my strength and my shield; my heart trusts in Him, and He helps me. My heart leaps for joy, and with my song I praise Him. The Lord is the strength of His people, a fortress of salvation for His anointed one."

PSALM 28:7-8

"Be on your guard; stand firm in the faith; be courageous; be strong."

1 CORINTHIANS 6:13

"God is our refuge and strength, an ever-present help in trouble. Therefore we will not fear, though the earth give way and the mountains fall into the heart of the sea, though its waters roar and foam and the mountains quake with their surging."

PSALM 46:1-3

"The Name of the Lord is a fortified tower; the

righteous run to it and are safe."

PROVERBS 18:10

"The Lord Himself goes before you and will be with you; He will never leave you nor forsake you. Do not be afraid; do not be discouraged."

DEUTERONOMY 31:8

"I keep my eyes always on the Lord. With Him at my right hand, I will not be shaken."

PSALM 16:8

"But He said to me, 'My grace is sufficient for you, for My power is made perfect in weakness.' Therefore I will boast all the more gladly about my weaknesses, so that Christ's power may rest on me."

2 CORINTHIANS 12:9

"No temptation has overtaken you except what is common to mankind. And God is faithful; He will not let you be tempted beyond what you can bear. But when you are tempted, He will also provide a way out so that you can endure it."

1 CORINTHIANS 10:13

"He gives strength to the weary and increases
the power of the weak."

ISAIAH 40:29

"Surely God is my salvation; I will trust and not be
afraid. The Lord, the Lord Himself, is my strength
and my defense; He has become my salvation."

ISAIAH 12:2

"Be strong and take heart, all you who
hope in the Lord."

PSALM 31:24

"It is God who arms me with strength
and keeps my way secure."

PSALM 18:32

"But the salvation of the righteous is from the Lord;
He is their strength in the time of trouble."

PSALM 37:9

"Seek the Lord and His strength;
seek His face evermore."

PSALM 105:4

"In the day when I cried out, You answered me,
And made me bold with strength in my soul."

PSALM 138:3

About The Author

Cassidy Glo Novak, has experienced just about every major trauma any person can, from childhood sexual abuse, a near-death experience, rejection, eating disorders, anxiety, anger issues, a broken marriage, and more. Through it all, she leaned into her faith and God brought her through every single tragedy. Today, Cassidy is the mom of five beautiful children, including identical triplets which she homeschools. She and her husband, Clif, live in Chicagoland where she loves to ride horses with her children on their small farm. Cassidy and Clif also enjoy public speaking and sharing their testimony while also helping to lead worship at their local church.

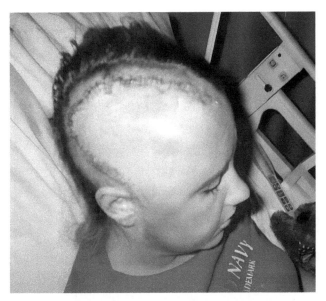

Starting rehab about a week after surgery.

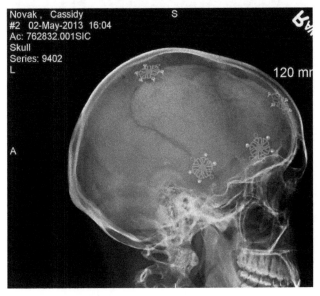

X-ray showing 5 plates and over 20 screws in my head.

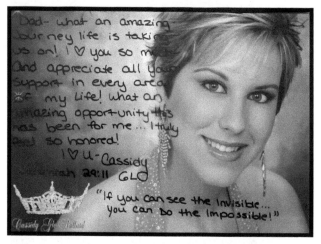

Miss Silver Springs 2005 headshot, 6 months after accident.

The night Clif and I met.

Photo taken by my sister on our rehearsal night.

Our beach ceremony, March 19, 2006.

The happy couple with Cassidy's grandparents.

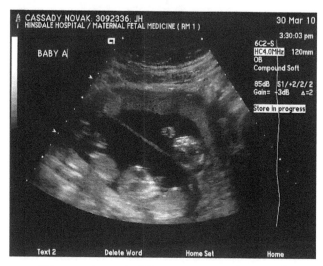

Ultrasound surprise! Not one...not two...but three!

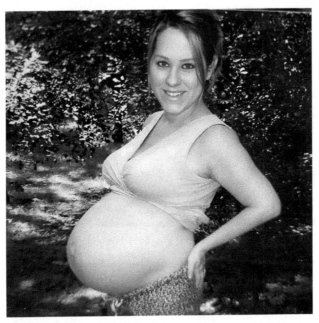

Not quite full term yet.

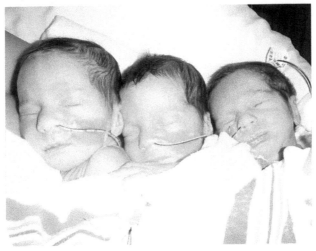

Cadence, Chloe, and Cailyn arrive August 29, 2010.

A quiver full on day 1! Finally, everyone is home.

Hands and heart full.

Cora's arrival September 18, 2015.

Clayton joins our bunch May 4, 2018.